Missionary, Go Home?

Missionary, Go Home?

by
Les Pederson

MOODY PRESS
CHICAGO

Library of Congress Cataloging in Publication Data

Pederson, Les, 1920-
  Missionary, go home?
  1. Missions—Influence.   I. Title.

BV2063.P35   303.4'82   80-14445

ISBN 0-8024-4881-X (pbk.)

Printed in the United States of America

CONTENTS

PREFACE

In the past few years it has become popular to engage in the human rights controversy. The United Nations has a human rights commission geared to investigate the countries and organizations that are purportedly violating the policies agreed upon.

Missionaries are being blamed along with third world governments for destruction of the cultures and value systems of some of the tribal people.

Anthropologists have joined in the fight. Their journals carry articles that discredit fundamental tribal missions. Many articles and a few books have been written, accusing missions of disturbing tribal culture and work. The authors differ in background. Some are reporters, others anthropologists, and some are novelists. Their credentials vary from no firsthand knowledge of the matter to those who spent a few days in the countries about which they have written. One author actually wrote a book on genocide in Paraguay without ever having been in the country. All of his information was secondhand at best.

Missionary, Go Home? is a documentary, written by the tribespeople themselves from many different countries around the world. Those men and women tell in their own words what it was like to live in paganism; about the fear, witchcraft, war, killings, and hopeless conditions in which they lived. They then testify to the result of the preaching of the gospel of the Lord Jesus.

Testimonials were recorded on tape in the native languages and translated by local missionaries into English. The tribal people "tell it like it is." The book gives the native himself a hearing, at the same time coming to the defense of missions.

7

ACKNOWLEDGMENTS

To all who have made this book possible, my deepest thanks. They are missionaries who labor in some of the remotest areas of the world, spreading the gospel of Jesus Christ among tribal people who live in jungle darkness. They are people who have learned the tribal languages and cultures and are competent to translate the testimonies of the individuals who share their stories with us.

We are truly grateful to the following people who responded and cooperated in our request for help and submitted the material used in this documentary:

Don and Pat Barger
Doug and Wynona Caulder
Fred and Barbara Findley
Bob and Mary Garland
Carol Gutwein
Gene and Nancy Gutwein
Norman and Linda Keefe
Helmut and Doris Keller

Fred and Virginia Pennoyer
George and Gwen Pierce
Joe and Jana Price
Fred and Ruth Sammons
Dan and Diana Shaylor
Tom and Darla Steffen
John and Lynne White
Tim and Betty Wyma

1

LEAVE THEM ALONE

The night was dark. The only light that existed was the eerie flickering of a fire from a nearby Indian hut. Occasionally we turned on our flashlight for a split second to get a better view of what was doing on, hoping we were not intruding too much into a ceremony in which we did not belong.

Our missionaries had started working with the Manjúi tribe a few years earlier. The tribe is located in an isolated area in northwestern Paraguay. Blindness, much from birth, some incurred later, seemed to be more prevalent in this group than in any other we had ever visited.[1] None of us spoke their language yet, and their culture was strange; but the people were friendly.

Just a few feet in front of us something strange was going on. We understood neither what they said nor what they were doing. We were witnessing a ceremony of some kind, but we did not understand it. An Indian woman was lying on her side on the ground. The dim fire lit up the area in ghostly fashion. We then saw a witch doctor or two bending over the woman, chanting in singsong voices, then spitting on their hands and proceeding to rub her seminaked body.

Everyone was sweating from exertion, plus the fact the evening was a bit warm. When one reached exhaustion, another moved in to carry on. All the while it appeared that no one was aware that we were even there. At any rate, no one seemed inhibited because of our presence.

We whispered to each other from time to time, not wanting to be rude or interrupt their ritual. Was she sick? Were the men trying to cure her? It seemed they were talking to spirits, but we could not be sure, because we did not speak or understand their language.

However, one thing was clear: those people were frustrated, worried, and frantically wearing themselves out trying to communicate with the spirit world or whatever, looking for help. What a sad picture. If only we could intelligently communicate and tell them of the love of God; if only we could share Jesus Christ with them. For the present, that was

---

1. Physical deformities, perhaps from inbreeding, accounted for much of the blindness. Some people even had no eye sockets. We also saw one baby on whose eyes the parents had put blueing.

11

impossible. It would take time to learn how to communicate. Meanwhile all we could do was pray. One thing impressed us about the Manjúi—they were not happy.

The occasion brought back to my memory an incident that took place in the United States. I thought, *How could anyone say, "Leave them alone; they're happy the way they are"? Why do intelligent people make such remarks? They are usually uninformed, but why don't they investigate before making such a ridiculous statement? Why aren't they here, right now, to see just how "happy" the Manjúi are in their pagan culture?*

I had been asked to give an invocation at a banquet where there were about a thousand guests in attendance. I was not sure just what was expected of me. Not wanting to throw the ceremony into chaos, there was only one thing to do. The people were all standing; the lights were out but for the spotlight on the Stars and Stripes and the podium; then I was introduced as the "reverend" who was going to say "grace." I stepped up to the podium with mixed emotions. It was one of the most uncomfortable situations I had ever been in.

Lord, I prayed, *help me to say something to these people, to make them think.* So, I opened by mentioning our years of labor in Paraguay, South America, among two tribes of people. I told how those people responded to the gospel, then made an application to heathen in America who needed the same gospel. I thanked the Lord for the food and sat down.

No doubt some of the guests and officials were relieved and others a little upset, but I was not quite prepared for the reaction of the gentleman who was sitting at the speakers' table to my left. His first remarks were, "Why don't you missionaries stay home and leave the natives alone—they're happy the way they are."

I was caught off balance for a few seconds, then responded by asking among which tribe he had worked. A plus for him is the fact that he did get embarrassed and stammered that he had not worked with any tribe. "I believe that, sir," I said. "No one would make such a statement if he had any firsthand knowledge of tribal people, no matter where they live." With that the communication between us broke off.

I need to correct that statement of fifteen years ago. There are people who visit various countries and tribal peoples and return to their home countries only to make the same statement: "Leave them alone—they're happy the way they are." Unfortunately, many of those people stay only a few hours, and at best a few days, circulating from one tribe to another in a third-world country. They cannot communicate with the people, and unless an honest interpreter is available, they leave with a warped idea of what they have seen.

A group of anthropologists gathered together in Barbados in 1971, under the auspices of a European university and financed by the World Council of Churches. The meeting was called to discuss ethnic friction among tribal people in Latin America.

The declaration made at that time, as a result of the conference, left no doubt as to the intent of the meeting.[2] Missionaries, called imperialists and colonialists, were blamed along with various governments for the plight of the tribal people.

To rid the tribes of that so-called negative influence, the group's recommendation was to send the missionaries home and replace them with "qualified" people who would meet the needs of the native people. The document was the first of many articles published, smearing the missionary.

Dr. Mark Munzel of the University of Frankfort, West Germany, wrote his findings in a European journal.[3] His work encouraged Norman Lewis, of the *Times* of London, to investigate.[4] The large newspaper published a detailed article, with pictures in full color, telling of atrocities perpetrated among the Aché tribes in eastern Paraguay, putting some of the blame on the missionaries as well as the Paraguayan government. The editorial was sold to many magazines and newspapers in several languages around the world.

More recently a book, *Genocide in Paraguay*, was written by a professor of law from one of our American universities in the east.[5] That man wrote about something he had no firsthand knowledge of—he wrote without having been in the country himself.

Later the man went to Paraguay, at the invitation of the Department of Defense, to see for himself that he was wrong. After he returned to the United States, he did indeed write another article, but not one of commendation. In effect, his opinion was that things were worse than he had heard.

In 1978 a film was made in Venezuela regarding Maquiritare Indians in the Amazonas department on the Orinoco River. The purpose of the film was to discredit the New Tribes Mission, and the producers had

2. "The Barbados Declaration," Conclusions of The Symposium Regarding Interethnic Controversy in South America, Barbados, January 30, 1971.
3. Mark Munzel, "Genocide in Paraguay," International Work Group for Indigenous Affairs (Denmark), 1972.
4. Norman Lewis, "Manhunt," *Sunday Times* (London), January 26, 1975.
5. Richard Arens, *Genocide in Paraguay* (Philadelphia: Temple University Press), 1977.

13

found a disgruntled Maquiritare man who would cooperate. Quite a few Maquiritares happened to be in Puerto Ayacucho where the film was shown. When it was over, the Maquiritares who had seen the film stood up and publicly denounced it as a pack of lies before all those present.

The articles, the books, and the film present the tribesmen as being content, happy, and enjoying life in their pagan state. They portray the missionary as a tyrant who moves into villages and imposes Western civilization, forcing tribespeople to change and embrace the Christian religion. "Leave them alone. They're happy the way they are."

The statement is not true. They are *not* happy; they live in fear of most everything from tigers to spirits. No one can really be happy without knowing Christ as Savior. It is for that reason I believe this book must be written. I have asked our missionaries to capture, with the tape recorder and in writing, actual testimonies from the tribal people themselves.

Some of the stories were taped during regular meetings when the Christians of the tribe gathered together. The missionaries have translated the testimonies into English from the tribal tongues, leaving the reproduction as much as possible as it was given. The translator has provided the English equivalent of some words in parentheses. A word-for-word translation would not be understood, whereas a dynamic translation or equivalent is meaningful.

The testimonies of those men and women tell what it was like to be pagan. They give us a peek into cultures in which their people have lived for centuries. Each person has something different to say, yet there is one common theme: All of them lived in fear. They were not happy running, roaming the jungle, looking for food. Fleeing from their enemies did not bring happiness or peace. Though those people come from the four corners of the world and speak different languages, they now have one thing in common—they have responded to the gospel of Jesus Christ and now are bound for heaven.

Are they happy the way they are? Should we let them alone? Let the people speak for themselves.

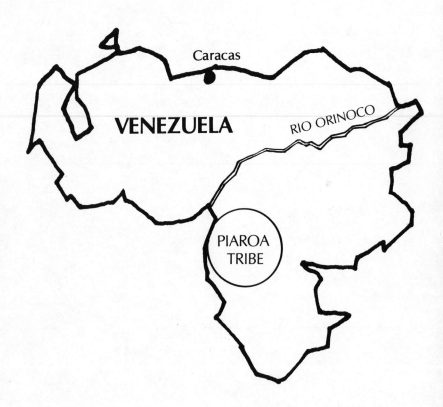

2

PIAROA TRIBE

VENEZUELA

The Piaroa tribe has a population of about five thousand. The people live in an area of about fifty square miles, in the southern part of Venezuela. Their small isolated villages average twenty to forty people each, and most are located on small streams that flow into larger rivers. Most villages consist of one family unit, that is, father, sons, sons-in-law, and so forth.

Each village has its respective captain and witch doctor, in most cases two different people. The captain is respected for his knowledge and ability to lead his people, but usually it is the witch doctor who has the most influence in decisions.

The Piaroas are not fighting people, but on the contrary are very peaceful and gentle. Any disagreement between them that is not settled by word-of-mouth or argument is settled by witchcraft. One of the parties involved goes to the witch doctor and asks him to cast some kind of spell on the other person. The spells often result in sickness or sometimes even death. The Piaroas are very strong believers in witchcraft, and when they think or hear of a spell being cast upon them, they immediately become afraid and often will go to another witch doctor and ask him to counteract the spell.

Time after time we have seen people die within several days of hearing about such a spell. The victims will apparently be in good health but then begin to act strange and fearful, and no amount of doctoring will help them.

In their own way, the Piaroas are religious people, but their religion is based upon what is taught by the witch doctor. All of their ceremonies have to do with some form of evil spirit worship, and their "creator" is a large animal called the *tapir*. They worship that animal and will have nothing to do with killing or molesting it in any way.

When missionaries first began working with the people (in the late 1940s), the Piaroas were very afraid of a white person. They would let

17

the missionaries stay in their villages, but were not receptive to the teaching for a number of years.

In the early years of the work it was necessary to learn their language in order to communicate with them properly. The Piaroas were very helpful in teaching the missionaries their language.

Now we have seen the Lord's blessing upon that work. Fifteen churches have been established among the Piaroas. Many of the churches were established by the Piaroas themselves, taking the gospel to their own tribespeople.

The first draft of the complete New Testament has been translated into the Piaroa language. Work is now being done on the final revision of the New Testament before printing. We count it a privilege to be involved in this work.

JUAN DIAZ

At first we lived without thinking at all about God. Because of that, we did only the things our forefathers told us to do. We really did not know about God; we believed in *Huajare,* the one our forefathers said made all the mountains, lakes, and everything. But I thought, "Is this really the truth?" We drank whiskey, sniffed dope, and stuck the stingray's barb through our tongue. Doing those things, we did know not the Word of God.

We were unhappy when we drank, sniffed dope, and fought with our friends. When we did those things we had no good feeling in our inner being. We were unhappy doing the things of this world: drinking, fighting, putting spells on our friends, and listening to and learning the chants.

Then I said to God, "My Father, I want You to come into me; they say that only You help us; I want to believe." When I told my father this, he did not answer; he did not hear [understand] me. I then said, "I am going to go on chanting; I don't know where God's Word came from."

As I became close to God, I knew that what our forefathers told us was only bad. Then I said to my father again, "Let's believe in God; the spirits don't help us." Then my father said, "Let's believe; it's true that the spirits and the chants and the special rocks do not help us." When he said that, I was really happy.

I said to him, "It is true that God lives; only He takes care of us when we eat other foods; only He watches over us." After that I entered into the belief of God. Although my father did not yet believe, I was happy because I was separated from the devil. Later my father believed, and we have both been saved from that evil. I say to my people, "Let's not go back to that; let's always follow God; we are very happy now."

In the beginning we only believed in bad things. We were told not to eat howler monkey, and we did not eat it. We were told not to eat wild pig until it had been chanted for, and we did not eat it. When babies were born, they would say, "We have not chanted, so you cannot eat birds." We lived dangerously and were continually afraid.

Also, when our children would die, others would say, "The spirit people are doing bad [evil]." When another man's child would die, we would say, "The spirits' spell killed him." Thus, doing those things, we arrived at what we believed. We lived very bad [sinfully]. After we

19

threw away what our forefathers did, and believed and were born of God, we are living happily now. Therefore, I tell my people, "Don't believe those things [former beliefs]; they don't count nowadays."

Our forefathers also told us not to eat the tapir. They called the tapir "our grandfather." They said he made this earth, the rivers, the mountains, the stars, the sun, and the moon. They said he made the birds, the food, and everything in the world. We believed what they told us.

At other times when we would go on the trails alone, they would tell us, "Be careful and don't let the spirits kill you." When we went out at night they told us that the tiger would get us. The children did not talk or play at night; they said the devil would answer the children, and it was dangerous. Since we have arrived at believing in God, living in the place where God is, we are not afraid; we go out at night and play, and all say that they are very happy now.

Before, when one got a snakebite, we would only chant for him; when someone was sick, we would chant for him. That is what we trusted in before—our forefathers believed this way. I said, "Can this be true?" Although I believed in God, I did not know anything about God at first.

When I would hear my father chanting, he would say, "We are a dying people," and I would think, "How did we become the dying people?" My father taught me that in the beginning *Huajare* and his brother-in-law *Purune* fought together. "How did the people begin?" I asked. He said, *"Huajare* fished them from a hole, and when *Purune* saw them he took them away. After *Huajare* made the Piaroas, he fought with the spirit that helped him create them, so now the spirit chastens the Piaroas, making them the dying people." That is what my father taught me, and I believed what my forefathers taught.

After I believed in God, I learned that God made Adam and Eve from dirt, and that we truly were dying people. I was happy to learn that. It was like taking something that has disappeared from sight and being found again.

Then I said to myself, "This is truly the beginning; what my father taught me was not true. God made everything; he made man and woman. My forefathers taught lies because they taught the teachings of the devil." Thus I believed in God. Now when they drink, sniff dope, and chant, I don't believe [in] it. Now when we dying people die, it will be good. There will be no bad [evil], and we will go where we will never die again.

I don't do what we used to do because it is not the truth; and even when I did it, I was not happy. I tell my friends that those things are wrong. I tell them that they cannot find everlasting life by taking dope and doing all the old things. We have heard that the fire awaits us when we do those thingcs. We are saved from the fire by believing in God.

When someone puts a spell from the alligator or the water snake, we are afraid, but God is stronger than those and has saved us from them. I continually tell my people to think about the things of our Creator and God. We can live happily that way. I tell them when someone tells us that the spirit is going to get us, we are not afraid, because God takes care of us; we are in His hands, and now we can live happily and without fear.

Juan Diaz's father, Juancho, was one of the main witch doctors and a village captain on the Parayquazu River, Amazonas, Venezuela. When Fred Findley and Santiago (a Piaroa Christian) first went into that area, their lives were threatened in Juan's village. As Juan said in his testimony, he first, and then later his father, accepted the Lord. Juan has been a real blessing and is respected by his people. He is in his mid-twenties and is a deacon of the church at Angelito. Juan is one of the four informants Fred Findley and Mary Lou Yount are using for the revision of the New Testament. He really loves that work and has said he wants to stay with it until the New Testament is finished.

3

PANARE TRIBE

VENEZUELA

The work of New Tribes Mission among the Panare Indians began in 1972. The tribe is located in Bolivar State, south of Caicara del Orinoco. That area is bounded on the north by the Orinoco, on the west by the Caura, on the south by the Chivapure, and on the east by the Suapure rivers.

From the beginning, our efforts at teaching literacy have been concentrated in the Colorado; however, the Panares themselves have extended the teaching to other areas as well. They are highly motivated in their desire to learn. For example, Mainan, Vicente Correa, from Turiba, visited the Colorado from time to time in 1975. He learned to read and write from other Panares while there. As he was learning, he went back to Turiba and taught the Panare men there how to read and write. He now has built a schoolhouse and continues teaching.

Other men from Colorado and Turiba have taught Panares in other villages. As a result there are a total of 111 Panare readers. Sixty-eight more men and 25 women are learning at present. After the Panares have a sufficient amount of practice reading and writing their own language, we help them learn to read and write Spanish.

Another dimension of our work among the Panares is the spiritual. Ever since missionaries first went to live among them and learn their language, the Panares have had a hunger to learn about God. In order to meet that need and to be obedient to our Lord, we are continuing to teach them God's Word. Each village has its own meetings three or four times a week in one of the village homes. They have four songs in their language now, which they sing at their meetings. They pray, read from their Bible storybooks, and the leaders (whom we are teaching in a small group) teach new stories they are learning.

Our ultimate goal is to translate the New Testament into the Panare language and establish functioning indigenous churches. The book they presently have includes the creation, Fall of man, Flood, and also includes briefly the gospel story. We are presently working on another on the life of Christ.

Generally speaking, the Panares are a healthy and hard-working people. They grow rice, ocumo, yuca, corn, mapuey, pineapple, payaya, and all kinds of eating and cooking bananas. They hunt and fish for meat, using spears made out of machetes, blowguns, and shotguns, and supplement their diet with wild fruits. Their main meal is eaten in the evening, after they return from hunting or working in their gardens. Everyone in the village eats together—the men in one group and the women in another.

The Panares build their houses out of palm extending from the peak to the ground, serving both as roof and walls. Recently, however, some have begun to buy tin because it is a lot of work to get new palm every two or three years.

The women spin cotton to weave loincloths, baby-carrying straps, and hammocks. Those are dyed red with onoto from their gardens. They also paint themselves with onoto when they want to dress up as a visitor or for a fiesta.

The Panare men specialize in basket making. They make guapas, deep baskets, and covered baskets from reeds they get in the mountains. Some reeds they paint red or black, and others they leave the natural color. They weave many designs into their baskets, as well as figures of people and animals. The Panares sell to tourists, and take their baskets to Caicara and as far as Ciudad Bolivar to sell them. With the money they buy sugar, salt, bicycles, radios and tape recorders, mosquito netting, machetes, axes, knives, pots, and so forth.

The Panares have always feared childbirth because so many have died in labor in the past. However, with help from our medical dispensary none have died in childbirth since we have been in the Colorado. As a result, fear is reduced, and the population is increasing. They are also improving in their hygiene, using soap and being more careful about their drinking water.

The Panare world view is animistic in nature and involves fear of evil spirits more than worship of a god. Even death itself is attributed to spirits rather than to natural causes. Fear has caused much heartache, sickness, and death in the past. But Christ died to "deliver them who through fear of death were all their lifetime subject to bondage" (Hebrews 2:15).

Fear is a very predominant theme of the Panare culture. They constantly nag their children, telling them to do this or that. The reason for nagging is often based upon a fear of injury to the child, but many times upon just a desire for obedience. The nagging is done by threatening the child or warning it of some impending catastrophe. One constantly hears such things as, "The spirits will get you if you do that," or the tigers, snakes, stingrays, and so on. It is such a habit that the Panares hardly talk to children without those warnings. Often even the missionaries are used as the boogeyman.

Ever since the missionaries first went to live among them and learn their language, the Panares have had a hunger to learn about God.

NAJTA

Before the Panares were paid for (saved), they used to say: "Sit down, kids, there are spirits around here." That's what they used to say before they were paid for. "There are spirits around here, there are spirits of the dead here." "Be quiet, there are tigers around," the Panares used to say, before they were paid for by Christ. "There are spirits of living Panares here that want to hurt us." They told their children to get into their hammocks so they would not make noise. The Panares used to say to their children: "Don't play; get in your hammock; don't fall down and die."

The Panares used to be afraid. They were afraid their children would fall down and die. They were afraid the spirits would come and bite them if they heard the children making noise. They said, "Don't fall, don't get hurt, put up that thing your're playing with, put up that knife, don't fall on it." They didn't let their children get injured because it was ugly to be injured. They were afraid of the spirits of the dead.

This is no longer so. The missionaries have told us there are no spirits of the dead. God says there are none, they said. The Panares said, "Is that true, there aren't any?" Today the Panares aren't afraid, they aren't afraid at all. They are happy now, they are strong, they don't get scared. They aren't afraid of the spirits of the dead or of the spirits of the living; they aren't afraid of the snakes or the tigers. They are strong; they are *paid* for now. This is what the Panares are like now. They are people who are not afraid.

(It is not that they are never afraid, but that the constant overshadowing fear is gone.)

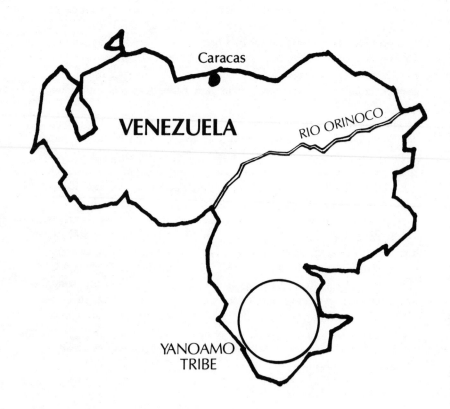

Caracas

VENEZUELA

RIO ORINOCO

YANOAMO
TRIBE

4

YANOAMO TRIBE

VENEZUELA

The Yanoamo people of the Parima mountains were contacted in May 1968 by missionaries of New Tribes Mission of Venezuela. They had been spotted a few years earlier in an aerial survey, and the plane had buzzed the valley where a number of naked Indians were seen running on the grasslands. Both the occupants of the plane and the inhabitants of the valley were excited at the encounter; but not all the commotion on the ground had been caused by the little red Cessna. Tribal warfare had just erupted, and the arrival of the plane had interrupted round one of what was to be a long battle, Yanoamo-style.

The missionaries made plans to return, but it was not until 1968 that sufficient personnel made the dream a reality. The trek had to be made by ground first. They followed a map that the aerial surveyors had drafted, and once an airstrip was cleared on the grassland, two resident missionary families moved in. Both had learned the tribal language at a mission station on the fringe of Yanoamo territory and were able to communicate upon arrival.

The battle that had begun the day of the aerial survey had gained momentum, and ambush parties from both sides had made several raids against one another. Not all had been successful, but the deadly, six-foot arrows had found their mark with sufficient frequency to maintain a violent cycle of attack and counterattack.

The way of life seemed harsh to the missionaries, but the Indians accepted it as normal. Hatred and revenge were taught to the children methodically, and all boys grew to manhood with a sense of responsibility to "even the score" for deaths that had occurred long before. Except for the very old or the very young, no deaths were accepted as normal. No matter that a life was claimed because of snakebite, malaria, or other disease; someone was always charged with having cursed the victim, and revenge was sought. Death came often to the Yanoamo villages, and there were always fresh accounts to be settled.

The missionaries presented themselves as friends, but in the Indians'

29

eyes they did not act as friends would. They refused to help them kill their enemies and spoke out against witchcraft and warfare. The opposing views threatened to break into violence more than once, when war captains attempted to intimidate the missionaries into joining the raiding parties or loaning their shotguns; but at the same time, some were driven by an inexplicable urge to understand the missionaries' message that fostered such revolutionary concepts. Love your enemies? Even friends were not entirely above suspicion.

Background work was done in preparation for a future literacy campaign. The Indians were systematically introduced to the wonders of the printed page, and two things in particular they found intriguing. One was that a person could pass on his thoughts to another without speaking a word, if both knew how to read and write. The other was that once a message was written, it came out exactly the same no matter who read it; it had no personal variations depending on the reader. The usefulness of that knowledge did not become apparent immediately.

A large number of Indians began to express agreement with the message brought by the missionaries. They were fascinated by Bible stories and acutely aware of the fact that God's insight into human nature was very exact. It made them uncomfortable to think that one so powerful knew them so well. They shared their feelings with others and were warned to beware. A number of the Bible stories sounded like foreign versions of their own tribal mythology. Why should they have any reason to suppose that the foreign version was the correct one?

The conflict came to light one day when one of the missionaries showed them his big English Bible and explained how he had to read the Bible stories in his own language and then translate them into theirs, in order to teach them what God says. He did not know why that comment stirred such excitement until they explained that he had just solved their problem. If he was getting his Bible stories from a written source, that settled it. Written messages do not change. Their own stories must be the ones that had become twisted with age.

By the end of 1969, a group that included a village leader and witchdoctor had taken a brave step onto the narrow road that leads to life. They were convinced of the truth of the gospel and willing to trust the Lord not only with their ultimate salvation but with their present safekeeping as well. They put witchcraft and warfare behind them, partly because they realized God was stronger than either, and partly because of an innate understanding that light and darkness do not mix. And they trusted the Lord to protect them from enemy arrows.

They served the Lord with typical fervency, making full use of their privilege of praying and their responsibility of preaching. Their numbers grew as others saw the reality of God's power, and the effect of the gospel was felt in all of the surrounding villages. A truce was eventually made with the enemy village, and the people of the valley settled into a new way of life.

There is today a strong group of believers there, and smaller groups of less-taught believers in the encircling villages as well. They are growing in the Lord and in the understanding of His Word; but tribal tradition is still a strong force to be reckoned with. Because no outside law enforcement prevails in the area, each village is responsible for its own defense; and a nonaggressive policy is no guarantee that a strong defense is unnecessary. One rebel in the group can create havoc with the best intentions of the village and cause situations that pose a constant threat to the security of all.

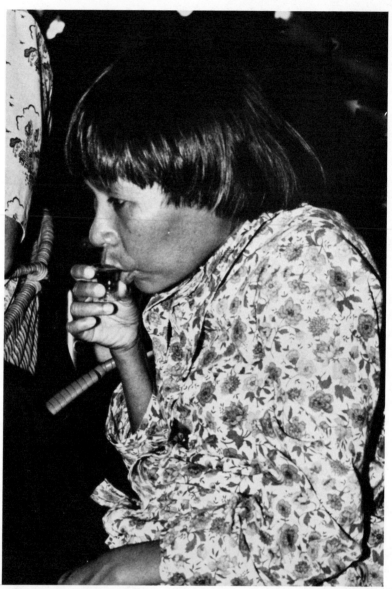
Dore–"Even though I can't see God, I believe in Him in my inner being."

DORE

Now I'm not sick anymore; I'm well. When I was a little girl, my mother lived with me in another village. While I was there those people put their magic herbs on me and I got very sick. I was sickly from then on; I didn't grow right. Now I'm well, and my inner being is happy and content too.

When I was sick I didn't eat. I didn't even eat the fruit they call *nao*. I was so sick that I became unconscious many times. But now I feel so much better. God has helped me and I'm not sick anymore.

It's obvious to me that God has helped me, and that helps me to trust God more. Even though I can't see God, I believe in Him in my inner being. I didn't eat meat, even when they killed some. When the foreigners first came I was afraid and didn't show myself.

Because I was so sick, the witchdoctors would try to make me better, but they never could, even though they tried many times. Now I know that only God can make a person better. When the witchdoctor would finish working over me, he would tell me I was better, but I didn't get better. Now I don't feel discouraged as before. My inner being feels alive and well now. I don't awaken with a headache and feeling weak now.

I was close to dying when the foreigners came with God's Word. Before God's Word came I just didn't know that God existed. When the foreigners told me about God and that He could make me better, I wanted Jesus. I began to feel better in my body and my inner being. My belief in God began to be strengthened.

One time when we were all living in the jungle and they were eating the fruit called *nao,* I became very, very sick. I became unconscious, and my family and the other Yanoamo thought I had died. Everybody gathered around me to cry. I became conscious again, sat up, and asked my mother what was going on. Even way back then God was watching over me.

I keep counseling the young women to follow my example and trust God to help them. Now those of us who are God's children are waiting for our older brother Jesus Christ to come and take us to His home. I want to go and live in God's home, but I'm sad because there are so many Yanoamo who don't know Jesus. I'm sad when I hear Yanoamo talking about fightings. They talk bad about my older brother, Enrique, when he tries to warn them not to fight. God doesn't want Yanoamo to fight. I warn my other brothers not to fight. I tell them that if you choose the old way of fighting and revenge, you'll end up dead, and then who will feed your widowed wife and children?

The Deceiver deceives people into thinking they are fierce, but then they just end up getting killed. I told my brother-in-law not to go with those other fellows to ambush the Balafili people, but he went anyway. He got himself shot in the leg with an arrow and now he can't walk, and who knows when he will get better? If he would have been killed, who would have taken care of his kids? I hope he won't be stubborn and go anymore.

ENRIQUE

Because God has helped me, I'm not afraid that other Yanoamo will shoot me. That's because I'm not unfriendly anymore and because I'm other peoples' friend now. Before, I used to say I was friendly, but now I really am friendly because God took away my hatred of people. Because God's Word is true and I want to have God's true Word in me, I don't hate people anymore.

Before, I used to think I was fierce, but I really wasn't; I was deceiving myself. God's Word is true and by God's power I'm able to resist getting all mad and fighting.

Before, even though I used to think I was fierce, I was afraid of snakes and our enemies. I know that killing someone isn't the way to be happy, because when you kill someone, you can be sure his relatives will be after you to kill you, till they finally do.

Jesus Christ has washed my inner being with His blood, and now I'm a saved one. Other Yanoamo tell me that it's not worth it to be friendly, because eventually they'll turn against you and kill you.

But I tell them that God will protect me. I counsel my brothers not to be afraid, because God is protecting us. I tell them not to be afraid, like others who aren't trusting God to help them.

Those who aren't trusting the Lord to protect them can't make big gardens because they're afraid they'll be ambushed while they work. Before God's Word came I was always afraid when I worked in my garden.

I used to think I wanted to be a witch doctor, and I was starting to be one, but then God's Word came and Jesus took the demons away. Even when I became God's child the demons would sometimes bother me and I would be afraid. Now it's been a long time since the demons have bothered me.

I keep teaching my children to follow God's way. I tell them there's no other way to live and be happy. Before the recent war between these two villages started, I made many trips telling them how to live in peace by following God's Word. Now they are fighting and I am sad.

I still want to go and teach other Yanoamo, but now everybody is fighting again and my people tell me not to go now. When there was that recent fight here on the savannah, I tried very hard to stop the fighting, so no one blames me for helping kill the man they clubbed to death.

Before God's Word came, my inner being was awfully dirty. I was always sneaking around through the jungle, trying to kill people by blowing on them with my magic herbs. Before God's Word came, when I was almost grown up, the demons came to me and deceived me. They made me think I could make people better when they got sick.

The demons can't keep you from the fire. Only God can save you and keep you from the fire. Even though I didn't have lots of brothers to accompany me on trips into the jungle to ambush and kill people, my brother-in-law and I would go by ourselves. I was sure I could, by my demons, make a big wind to come up and blow the trees so hard that no one could catch me after I'd shot someone with my arrows.

The Deceiver was leading me along, before God's Word came. I used to have an especially short stick with which I planned to kill people. I was going to hit them right between the eyes. Now when I think about how deceived I was, I say to myself that I used to be all messed up.

Before God's Word came we used to be hungry much of the time. We would quickly plant a little garden and then run off to some secret place in the jungle so our enemies wouldn't find us. The children would be hungry, and I'd feel bad.

Now it's so much better because I don't have to be wondering if there's an enemy behind every tree when I walk through the jungle. Now I have big gardens and feed many people. If God weren't helping me, I couldn't do it. Now my inner being is peaceful and happy, not like it was before I knew God, and we were always fighting.

Before I knew God, we used to blow drugs up each other's nostrils. We would go completely out of our senses. When I would take the drugs, I was hoping it would awaken the fierceness within me. But it never did. I was hoping I would become fierce like a jaguar, but I was just deceiving myself. I was going to be fierce and stab my enemies with my bamboo arrow points. I don't think that way now.

We eat so much better now that we have the strength to make big gardens. God has helped us make bigger gardens. Recently several villages that are fighting with other villages came to me for food. These people were very hungry and their gardens were all used up.

When people are fighting they don't make gardens and then they go hungry. It's because they are afraid to work in the gardens. Their children are hungry, but they don't have anything to feed them. If you have to be looking around all the time while you're working, you can't accomplish much. I don't want my children to go hungry ever again.

God is the one who gives us our crops. Before our crops didn't grow well, but now God is making them grow for us to eat. Because of all these things I trust God to help me, to protect me, and to make my garden grow. God *is* very good to us.

LEO

Before the gospel came, even though I didn't have fierceness in me, I thought I did. I went many times to blow a magic herb on my enemies, but I didn't kill very many. I went to try to shoot my enemies, the Shamatali. That was before God's Word came. I was very frustrated then. I didn't kill very many of my enemies.

My friends [missionaries] have brought God's Word. By God's Word we are content now. Before God's Word came, we Yanoamo didn't like each other. Even among our relatives we were unfriendly. We beat each other on the chest; we hit each other's hands with long poles.

Now we who live close to each other live peacefully together. We used to look for our enemies' footprints. We would gather the dirt that the footprint was on [in leaves] and work sorcery on the person.

Many times the person wouldn't die, that we had worked sorcery on. We used to say it was because the magic herbs were no good. My ancestors used to fight each other with poles. Nobody was ever satisfied with the results of the fights, and they'd have to fight each other again and again.

The Yanoamo called Shiitali used to come against us with magic herbs to blow on us to make us die. My nephew used to sneak around down by their villages, waiting for a chance to break their bones with an especially strong stick that he carried for killing people.

We used to be all the time beating each other on the chest with our fists. We never really felt satisfied. Now we feel good because we have God's Word where our inner being is. Before God's Word came, my inner being and my hands were dirty, because I was handling that magic herb with which we killed people. Before my friends came, we never even dreamed that God's Word existed. We hit each other and fought with each other. Jesus made my inner being clean, and I'm following after God.

Before we knew about God's Word, I was afraid our enemies would sneak up and shoot me, so I couldn't work in my garden. Because of that, we were hungry. I had just a little garden and we were always hungry. Now I don't have enemies, and I can work in my garden unafraid.

There are a few men from our village who have been persuaded to help those other Yanoamo ambush our former enemies. I'm afraid our former enemies will blame all of us because of those few from our village that went to ambush them.

I keep telling my sons not to get involved in hostilities. I tell them how we older men suffered. I keep telling my sons that they didn't help

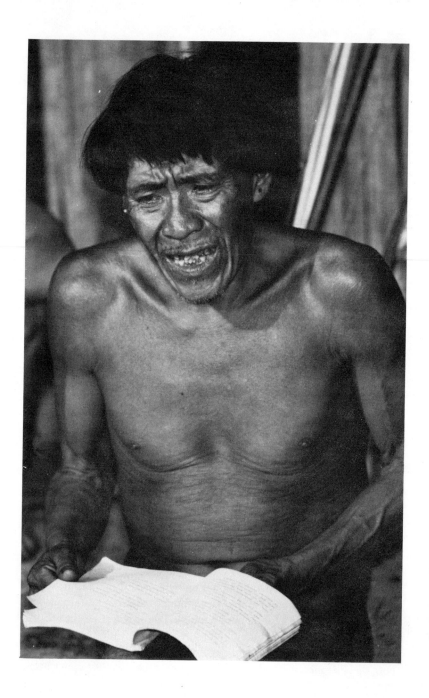

us when we needed help, so don't risk your life now for them.

My nephew and my niece keep telling me [reminding me] how God has given us lots of children, more than before. Right now, even though my tooth is hurting, I'm happy to be talking about God.

I asked my brother-in-law if he was following the Lord, and when he said no, I was very sad. I said to him that only God can protect us from those demons that used to bother us so much. Now, even though we can't see God, by His Word we know He exists and protects us.

I keep telling my son-in-law that God's Word is the good Word and that those who follow it will be happy. I keep telling myself not to get involved in hostilities, because they lead to unhappiness. I constantly tell my people that God's Word is the good Word and that we won't be disappointed if we follow God.

Before the gospel came, the demons were close to getting me. They had already almost made me so that I couldn't shoot game. At that time I didn't know what to do, but now Jesus has rescued me from the demons. Now I tell my sons that they should always follow God's eternal Word.

Before we heard God's Word we didn't know God, because we didn't know He existed. Now we know God exists and we obey His Word. We know that God made the forest, and He makes the food in our gardens get mature and ready for us to eat.

When we used to go on raids, and we would ask other Yanoamö to help us kill our enemies, we were always afraid that our enemies would ambush us. Some people from my village are afraid that our former enemies will come and try to ambush us again.

I tell them that if they trust God to save them, not trusting in arrows, God will turn them back before they get to our part of the jungle.

When visitors from other villages come to visit, I'm friendly to them and feed them, because I don't have unfriendliness in my inner being anymore.

"I'm happy to be talking about God." Leo, singing to the Lord.

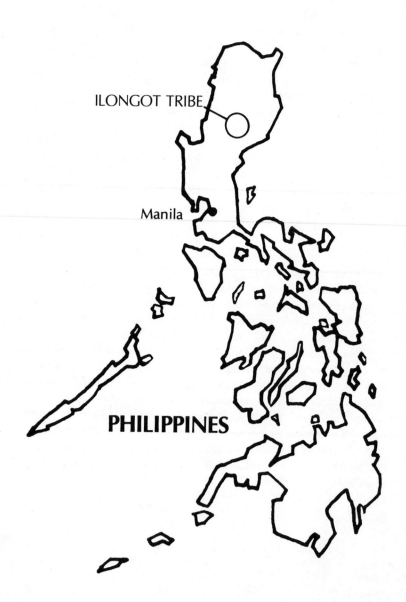

ILONGOT TRIBE

Manila

PHILIPPINES

5

ILONGOT TRIBE

PHILIPPINE ISLANDS

The Ilongot people of the Sierra Madre range of mountains on the island of Luzon, the Philippines, are a head-hunting group of people numbering approximately forty-five hundred people today. The mountainous area in which they live is about one hundred thirty miles almost due north of Manila. For many years the Ilongot were a secluded tribe, an isolated people, because their head-hunting activities tended to keep even the loggers and miners out of that area.

The people are a fairly stable group of farmers and hunters. Clearing the forest for their gardens is a huge job every year, but a necessary one. Their gardens produce rice, sweet potatoes, various vegetables, and fruit. The men are good hunters and have been able to keep their villages well supplied with meat. However, with the onslaught of pioneers in the area now, that will be an ever-increasing problem to them, as wildlife becomes less and less available to the Ilongot.

Pioneers in the area? Yes. Since the gospel of Jesus Christ came to the Ilongot people, many have been saved. The New Testament, which is soon to be completed, has given them God's word for their direction in life, and the believers have had a tremendous effect on the culture of the whole tribe. Head-hunting still goes on, but at a greatly reduced pace. "Therefore if any man be in Christ, he is a new creature: old things are passed away; behold, all things are become new" (2 Corinthians 5:17). Because of that, many lowland peoples have begun to migrate into the area, knowing the Ilongot is a changed man. Losing his land and freedom to the pioneers, the Ilongot is at a tremendous disadvantage, much the same as was the American Indian of the 1800s.

In spite of the physical disadvantage he faces, the Ilongot is growing spiritually, and the gospel is slowly advancing into every area of Ilongot country. Missionaries are still in evidence among them, but their work is one of teaching believers, encouraging the church, and pressing a literacy program upon the Ilongot, to bring the church to a vital reproductive place in its society, as believers read the Word of God for themselves and are taught thereby.

There are six churches today. Each church has its own pastors and teachers. There are many other small groups meeting, and the Holy Spirit is striving with all of them toward maturity in the Christian life. The churches have produced some evangelists who travel and teach and are supported by the church. Progress now is slow, as it simply takes time for Christians to grow in grace and in the knowledge of the Lord. It is really a time for rejoicing. Basic problems are over. There is no real hindrance to God's Word other than the individual's heart condition as God deals with him.

The Ilongot church will take on the problems of integration as more and more strangers come into the area. The missionary today is helping the Ilongot people prepare for the coming of all the modern world has to offer, some good and some bad. Loggers, miners, and pioneers have made deep penetration into the area, bringing with them all that the natural man can conjure up to do. The faith of the Ilongot will be tried, and God will prove Himself able to meet their every need in Jesus Christ. His Holy Spirit will guide and direct, comfort and sustain them even as He does for us.

DILANGYAW

Our bare feet made no sound as our head-hunting party approached the three grass-roofed houses built on the mountainside. We must be very quiet so that the guard dogs would not start barking and warn of our coming. We surrounded the houses, some guarding under the windows, others ready to push in the bamboo doors. Suddenly a dog barked, and immediately others joined.

At the same time, we rushed into the houses. I was first inside one house and saw a man reaching for his gun on the wall. I quickly hit him on the head with the back of my knife to stun him. Then I grabbed his long hair in one hand and whacked off his head with my very sharp head-hunting knife. All around me people were screaming in terror, but I felt only satisfaction that the head was cut off in one blow. I was not disgraced.

We took four heads that night. We felt this was good exchange for the heads these people had taken from our village some time ago. Before leaving the three houses, whose occupants had fled into the jungle, we cut the hands and feet off our victims. We would take these home for our young boys to play with, to condition them to become brave and not afraid to kill. We did not want our boys to grow up to be as women.

My own father began teaching me the head-hunting songs and dances when I was very young. At about nine years of age, he allowed me to go with him on a raid and helped me get my first head. How proud he was of me, but I noticed my mother was very quiet. No Ilongot wife or mother knew if her husband or son would return to the house whenever he left.

It was the dream of every Ilongot boy to be able to cut off a head so that he could wear the beautiful body-and-hair decorations showing that he was a true man. My father fashioned my head-hunting earrings from the beak of the hornbill, a large bird in our area. How proud I was to have my ears pierced at the top; then the long red earrings were fastened on, with their decorations of polished brass and spangles of mother-of-pearl shell.

Before we would go hunting, even for the wild deer and pig, we would often kill a rooster and sprinkle the blood on our guns and knives, chanting to the devil and the demons. Our lives were ruled by superstition and fear of the evil spirits.

Who would not fear the spirits who could do such miracles? For example, if some one had committed a sin against the tribe and would not confess, the test by boiling water was performed. In every case, the guilty one was found by this test.

The men of a certain village, or perhaps several villages, would gather together. A large cooking pot would be filled with water and brought to a rolling boil over a wood fire. Then the wood was pulled out from under the pot, so that the water just steamed. Now one by one the men passed by holding the palm of one hand over the water. As the guilty one's hand passed over the pot, the water would boil out all over the ground.

But in spite of our brave words and actions, our hearts were always filled with fear. Except in killing, in which we felt no fear, we were afraid of sickness, of evil spirits, of death. We never knew when we might be attacked as we walked the mountain trails, as we went to the river for water, or slept in our houses at night. We kept many dogs in all of our houses, used both for hunting and for guarding.

We watched our children die without medicine or any kind of medical help. We had schools only near the lowland. Our people were dirty, cruel, and worked just enough for a bare living.

Then into our mountains came people called missionaries. We heard how they lived in some of our villages. They brought medicine that would take away pain and fever; they taught both adults and children to read and write, and helped the people in getting basic supplies such as salt and soap. However, I heard that they taught strange things. They wanted us to stop killing. Why, we would all become as women! By this time I had taken so many heads I had long since lost count; I was the chietain of my village.

One day a missionary came to see me and asked if he and his family could move to our village. He promised to bring medicine, to teach our children to read, and to teach us about his God, who, he said, was much more powerful than the devil and the demons. I didn't want anything to do with his God, but it might be good to have the medicines. I agreed. The missionary built a house and an airstrip. I just observed him. If necessary, I could easily kill the missionaries.

Soon the family, with a baby girl, were settled in our village. We would go there and beg for anything we could see. We would sit around their table and wait for them to eat so we would get their food. We didn't help them in any way.

After three months, the husband left, and the wife and baby were left alone. My daughter, Demgak, liked this woman missionary, and she

44

asked if she and another girl could sleep in the missionaries' house at night so that the woman wouldn't be alone.

Soon we began to notice that Demgak was acting crazy. She didn't yell and become angry as she always had before. When we tried to find out what was happening to her, she would smile at us and say that she was learning good things from the Book the missionary's wife was reading to her. I was angry! This crazy missionary woman was making my daughter crazy. So I walked over to the house of the missionary.

I climbed up the ladder and roughly pushed the door open. The baby awoke and cried, but the woman asked me gently, "What do you want?" "Where is your husband?" I demanded fiercely. "He went to Manila last week and he may be gone a month. Why?" Angrily I told her, "We don't want you to stay here any longer. We don't believe what you teach about your God; it is all foolishness. What have you done to our daughter, Demgak? She comes here every afternoon, and when she comes home she tells us many things we don't understand. She is crazy now, and if she continues to come here, I'll kill her!"

I was surprised that the woman showed no fear, but answered me softly, "It was God who sent us here and we believe He wants us to stay. We do not force your daughter to come here; she wants to come, and we know that some day God will change you like He is changing your daughter." I was wondering about her answer, but I spit angrily on the floor and started down the stairway. "You fool; you are just wasting your time!" I said.

Later I discovered that Demgak, my daughter, had gone crying to the missionary after I shouted at her and hit her that afternoon. She was afraid I would kill the missionaries, but the missionary woman comforted her, and that night Demgak made friends with the missionaries' God.

When she came home in the morning we all noticed how different she was. We shouted at her and scolded her and hurt her, but she just told us, "If you will believe in the true God in heaven, then you will have peace and joy like I have, and then you will not hurt me anymore."

The next day I said to my family, "We have noticed that something good has happened to Demgak. We will go to the house of the missionary." I didn't know it then, but it was Sunday morning, and the missionary woman had just finished praying to her God. She looked out the window and saw all twelve of my family coming toward her house.

This woman could talk our language, and she seemed so happy to greet us and invite us into her house. "Are you wondering why we all came?" I asked. "We want to know why Demgak acts so crazy in a good way. She is very different now than she used to be."

I smiled at the missionary, and she saw that my body and loincloth were clean. Then the missionary got her Book and began to tell us about God and all that He created, how He created man in His own image, how man sinned against God. We were all very quiet as we heard these words.

Every day we went back to hear more about God from the missionary's Book. After three weeks I saw all my terrible sin, and I hungered for the forgiveness and cleansing of God. How I longed for peace in my heart!

So I surrendered my life to Jesus, God's Son who died to pay for my sins. I determined to serve Jesus and not Satan and the demons. Oh, as I thought of all those poor souls I had killed, I felt tears coming into my eyes. I could not stand the sight of my always shiny and sharp head-hunting knife. I would let it get dull by chopping wood.

My life was so different, with Jesus living inside me, that my wife and four of my children gave their lives to Jesus too. I cut my long hair as a sign that I no longer would cut heads and wear the head-hunting decorations. When the missionary man came back he asked me, "Why did you cut your long hair?" I answered him seriously, "Because I want to be a real man according to the Bible. It says that if any man be in Jesus, he is a new man; old things are passed away, all things are new." The missionary grasped my hand and answered me, "Oh, praise the Lord, my brother! You *are* a new man!"

Now, instead of begging, we have learned to give. Instead of cruelty, we have learned kindness. Instead of fear, we have peace. In many Ilongot villages there are native Christian churches, where Ilongot church elders teach our people. I, too, am a church elder. We have conferences every few months, some for the church leaders, some for the young people, and also a general believers' conference. We no longer fear the devil and his demons.

We can lie down at night now without fear of a raiding party killing us and our loved ones. Instead of raiding far-off villages, we go to tell them about Jesus. Until the day I go to be with Jesus, I shall be thankful that He sent missionaries to us.

"Now instead of begging, we have learned to give. Instead of cruelty, we have learned kindness. Instead of fear, we have peace."

DUMAGAT
TRIBE

Manila

PHILIPPINES

6

DUMAGAT TRIBE

PHILIPPINE ISLANDS

Thirty minutes north of Manila, flying in a small Super Cub airplane, one would already be over one of four Dumagat tribal areas. The Tagibulos Dumagat, numbering about two thousand are the southernmost Dumagat people. Next to them are the Kabulowan Dumagat, another language group, numbering five hundred. To the north along the east coast above Baler are the Casiguran Dumagat, about one thousand strong and of another dialect of Dumagat. Farther up the east coast along the Sierra Madre range of mountains are yet the Palanan Dumagat, about one thousand in number.

Those groups of people, so different in language, are yet one people called the Dumagat, the "people by the sea." Basically nomadic, the Dumagat seeks his food in the jungle and along the shallow waters of the sea coast. If one can call moving every week or so a simple life, that is the simple life they lead. Where one finds available natural food, one will find Dumagat people. When the food has been consumed, the people move on. It is a "stuff-and-starve" culture, difficult for everyone. It is survival of the fittest. Hence the Dumagat, though small, is a very strong person, able to seek a living out of the primitive jungles without ever really settling in one place. Home is where he makes his lean-to shelter for the night, and it is no problem to walk from it tomorrow.

The Dumagat is the same today as he was one hundred years ago. Governments have tried to settle him and educate him. Religions have had their say to the Dumagat, and yet he is unchanging. Today Christianity is reaching into the Dumagat areas and, as in every culture it touches, the good news of Jesus Christ is bringing salvation to the Dumagats. It is also bringing change to their lives. Many have settled in areas so they can be taught from the Scriptures. Many are learning to read so they can handle the New Testament that has been completed in two of the dialects, along with portions of the New Testament in another dialect.

The missionaries, though glad for the opportunities to teach, are also faced with bringing in new ways to make a living. The greatest advance has been with the Tagibulos people south of Baler, where a large church is located. The people have taken to farming and fishing, and the church is a visible, local entity having good effect up and down the coast.

Other areas inland are less stable—the Dumagat is still a wanderer. However, the Word of God goes with the Christian Dumagat and wherever he meets others he is a witness to the unsaved or to the Christian who enjoys the fellowship and teaching of others. In those areas the local assembly is not a visible entity other than the occasional meeting of Christian brothers and sisters in the Lord. God's Word is counted on heavily: "For where two or three are gathered together in my name, there am I in the midst of them" (Matthew 18:20). Will the church go forward in a culture like theirs? Will there be follow-up work for new believers? As long as Dumagats wander, they will continue to meet one another to share and to grow. Undoubtedly there will be a day, the Lord tarrying, that will bring the Dumagat together. But we do not see that day coming soon, and the missionaries are hard put to do what we would call a "successful church-planting work." God is doing His work in individual lives by His Holy Spirit, however.

ANGEL KATKAT

I was drunk almost daily. I was eating very little and only interested in *alak* [that is the name for any kind of alcoholic drink]. I had to pay for the *alak*.

The *abjang* [a name for every non-Dumagat, who are mostly traders] sold it to me and other Dumagats. At one time I even sold one of my daughters to the *abjang* for *alak*. But she always ran away and came back home.

I also own a small coconut plantation, but all the crop I had to give to the *abjang* because of my debts to him. Yes, I borrowed some food from him, but the big amount was for *alak*. I could not work much, because so many times I was drunk.

I also was very much afraid of the Libiongs [Libiongs are spiritual beings, mostly evil—to be feared]. Our people told us to be afraid. I do believe that they are there, because my parents and the old people told us so. They do give sickness. There are many of them and various kinds. Some live, for example, in the trees of the jungle, and others in the creeks. If you go hunting, you have to leave some meat along the trail, or they will be angry and you will not be able to hunt anything.

I remember one time, when I was still a boy, my father and I went hunting. He stepped on something sharp in the creek, and by evening his foot was very swollen and very painful. Quickly we called his father who knew how to *sobkal,* which is kind of a chanting, together with placing some ceremonies over a sick part of the body. Not long thereafter his foot was well again.

The Libiongs tell the people (in their dreams) what medicine to give. Not everybody can *sobkal*—this is done in a language not understood by other people. Yes, I know there are Libiongs, and many of them, all around us—I was very afraid of them.

Then one day the missionary came to our village. He could not speak our language yet; but I went there every night to listen to some plates [gospel recordings] that could talk our language. There I heard for the first time what the Bible says about many things, also about sin and Jesus Christ. I believed it and was very surprised to find out that the Bible knows so much about my own life, even the magic I had learned.

But now that I believe in Jesus and what the Word of God says, I don't use magic anymore. Also I'm no longer afraid of the Libiongs, and [since I first believed] I don't drink *alak* anymore; I do not need it now—it had only made me sick.

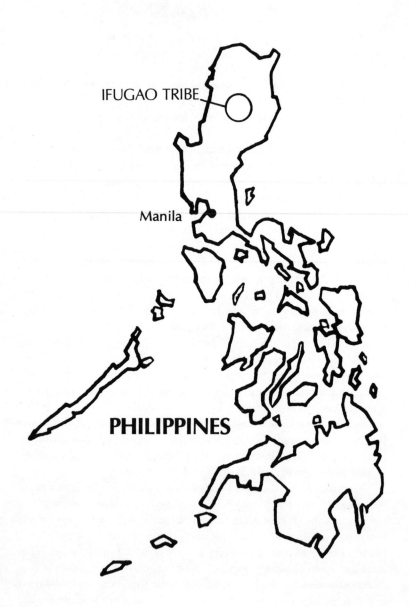

IFUGAO TRIBE

Manila

PHILIPPINES

7

IFUGAO TRIBE

PHILIPPINE ISLANDS

Tucked away in central Luzon of the Philippines lies one of the wonders of the world—the Ifugao rice terraces. From the bases to almost the summits of three-to-seven-thousand-foot mountains stretch the exotic, handcarved terraces. Philippine ethnologists tell us this "industrious race" originates from Malaya, pushed into the mountains by stronger Malayan immigrants. Whatever reason, their geographical isolation has played an important role in keeping their culture uninfluenced by outsiders over the centuries.

The Spanish later arrived and set up military posts and missions in several areas inhabited by Ifugao. For all their labors, very little was accomplished in civilizing or Christianizing these independent people. In the early 1900s under American occupation, head-hunting was terminated by force. Civilizing had begun, but it would still be years before Jesus Christ would be recognized by some as Savior.

Approximately one hundred fifty thousand Ifugao reside in Ifugao Province. Of the many different groups of Ifugao, this chapter deals with the southernmost group, the Antipolo/Amdugtug Ifugao. Their small geographical area is surrounded by three other peoples—the Kiangan Ifugao to the north, the Ayangan to the east and south, and the Kalanguya on the west and south.

A mountain range running almost north and south divides Antipolo and Amdugtug. The mountains also make a social division. The Amdugtug people consider themselves more sophisticated, as they reside closer to civilization—Kiangan. The Antipolo people were born on "the wrong side of the mountain."

The Ifugao do not have a political organization. That, however, does not mean they do not have a well-developed system of laws.

The family is the primary social and legal unit, consisting of ancestors, the living, and the yet unborn. Of the living, the children are the most important. The family exists for the benefit of the children. Husband and wife are considered to be of equal social and economic value.

What the Ifugao lacks in political organization he more than makes up for in his religion—one of the most extensive and pervasive systems in the world. Its cosmology divides the universe into five regions alive with some fifteen hundred deities. Those and their ancestors are placated continually by priests (*mabeki*) for two basic reasons—health and wealth. Numerous chickens, pigs, and water buffalo may be sacrificed at one time, depending on the nature of the sacrifice.

In 1962, Dick and Lou Hohulin of the Summer Institute of Linguistics (Wycliffe) moved into Napayo on the Antipolo side, residing there intermittently until 1971. Their job was to break down the language and translate the New Testament into that dialect. During their residence, periodic Sunday meetings were held where many came to hear and two or three became Christians. In 1972 we (Tom and Darla Steffen) moved into Dugyo, Antipolo under New Tribes Mission. Our job was to establish churches in the key areas.

The first baptism took place in 1973, with nineteen more the following year. The church was born. Two Batad Ifugao evangelists were used mightily by the Lord to help bring that about. The whole valley was in shock. How could anyone go against what the ancestors had taught? Other religious groups were furious and yet stunned. How could we get the Ifugao to stop sacrificing, something other missionaries had not been able to do for fifty years?

The great job of postbaptismal care was launched. Evangelism was stressed during that time, and the gospel leaped across cultural boundries into Ayangan. One factor that aided postbaptismal care was the Ifugaos' obsession to win an argument. To be defeated in an argument was proof one's belief was inferior. They had to have answers, and the Bible was studied vehemently to gain them.

Six men were ordained in 1977. Those men became the focal point of our ministry preparing them for our departure in 1979. We now continue an itinerant ministry with the church. In 1979 was also the birth of their first daughter church on the southern border of Antipolo.

PABLO CUYAHON

When we were not believers, this is the way in which we were married. We became engaged by a sacrifice that was provided by my family. The sacrifice was five big pigs. After that was over and some time had passed, we harvested rice at my wife's field. Many people came from all over to help in the harvesting.

We sacrificed another smaller pig, then went to my field and did the same thing. Time passed and things did not go well, and we separated. I later married again, doing the same sacrifices. After a long sickness my second wife died.

If we have someone die, we have to get blankets, skirts, especially we who are rich—we have to get double of everything used when someone dies. If we have pigs, these will be sacrificed so she can take their spirits to the ancestors. If we have no pigs, we are forced to get some, because for three days five big pigs and one water buffalo will be used.

If someone dies, we are forced to get everything that is needed; even if you have none, you are forced to get it. If you do not give enough to the ancestors, someone else in the family will die. Her ghost will come back and call someone. Many times we have heard ghosts walking around.

When there is someone dead and the dogs bark, that is a sure sign that a ghost is around. We do not want to go with the ghost, and that is why we must get everything that is needed for the sacrifice.

What was really fearful was after an animal had been sacrificed, the *shaman* would look at the gallbladder. If he said it was the wrong shape, we knew someone would die. We would have to get another pig and sacrifice it; then if the gallbladder was good, we would be OK. That is what we feared before we believed the Jesus way.

Some time passed, and I heard and listened to God's Word; it sounded good. Many of the things I heard corresponded with what our fathers had told us. Then they said that there was going to be a conference to study the Bible at a far-off village to which none of us had ever been. It took us three days to get there. We almost came back because we got lost and did not have anything to eat. I know now that it was God who kept us going.

There at the conference many taught the Bible. What really surprised me was that there were old man like me who were teaching.

They had stopped sacrificing and they had not died, and now they were teaching the Bible. It was during that time that I understood and believed. As for me now, I gave up the old way. I have caused my mind to be new. There is no more of the old way for me. Even for harvest we do not sacrifice anymore. We have removed the sacrificial system.

Even if we have someone who is sick, we only trust God to make him better. Jesus Christ is the one who gave us the power to remove the old way. We believe His power is very strong. He is the one we trust daily for our sicknesses, sleeping, and traveling. If we die, we no longer have fear, because we will go with Him, as He paid for our sins.

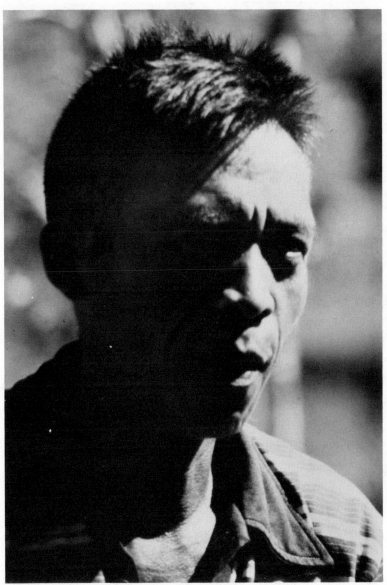

"As for me now, I gave up the old way."

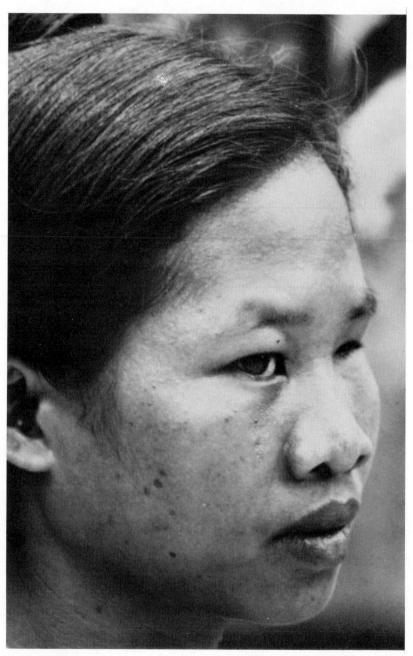

"Our hope is great now that we have believed–but before, none at all."

AGINAYA TAYABAN

I will tell how our life was before we believed and about our life after we believed. When we were small, it was then Father was still living. We had many problems during that time; it was really rough; we were oppressed by our fear of death. It was at that time that Father was sick.

We continued to offer sacrifice to the spirits and the ancestors because we thought they might accept them and Father might live. After a long time Father died. We had spent much; we suffered a great deal. We mortgaged one of our rice fields because of the animals we had to buy to sacrifice so Father could take their spirits to the world of the ancestors.

We had incurred many debts for all the chickens, pigs, water buffalo, blankets, and other things used in the sacrifices for Father. After a while we were getting all of our debts paid off and our rice field back, when the sickness transferred to Mother.

For a long time she was very sick. Until her death we had spent very much, so were very oppressed. We sold a rice field to pay for the sacrifices we do for death, because we did not have any money. But, we were forced to get the money for sacrifices so that Mother's spirit would not come back to call us to go with her. If we did not, she would remember and come back.

When that was over, we brothers and sisters became sick. It was then that we were really fearful, because we had in our minds that all of us were probably going to die. Why did our parents die and now the sickness was transferred to us? Because of our customs, our problems were enormous.

After a while Tom Steffen came; God sent him to cause the Jesus way to be known. He taught the Jesus way, but I did not believe it. Alonzo, my brother, was the first to understand the Jesus way and wanted to believe, but I did not believe. I was still thinking of our customs, because that was our way. How could our customs ever be removed?—that's our way.

We continued to study the Bible, God's Word. I came to understand about salvation, but was still uncertain in my mind; my mind was very distressed. I thought, how could the old customs be left? It seems like we will have to follow both ways, our old customs and the Jesus way. They said that was not possible. I thought [meditated] daily [so] that I could settle my mind to follow only one way.

After a while the Dick Hohulins came to visit and brought with them two Ifugao evangelists from an Ifugao tribe up north. Then at that time it was like my mind settled on one way, and my brother and I were baptized. It was at that time that we left the customs we had followed for so long.

Several months passed and then one of my brothers was persuaded to join us believers. Our family is six. Several years passed and two more joined us, the oldest and the youngest. We are now following the Jesus way and have neglected the old customs.

Now, as I think of the difference of the Jesus way and our old customs of sacrifice, the difference is very great. Our customs that we believed in before were very difficult; we had no peace; we were afraid to die—we did not know the Jesus way.

We did not know Jesus, and we did not know that we were sinners. We knew there was a God, but we did not know His way; we had no peace at all then. Even though we had the sacrifice system to trust in for removing our sicknesses, it was only sickness that we thought about removing by sacrifice; we did not know the way of salvation, the way Jesus can cause us to be saved.

Our thanks are many now since we have believed. Our happiness is great now because we have peace. We know now that we are sinners and that Jesus died for our sins; we know that we are saved; we also know whom we have placed our trust in. We are not afraid to die, because even if we get sick and die, we will be better off, as our spirit will go to the place of God. Those are the reasons the difference is great between our life before we believed and now.

Our hope is great now that we have believed—but before, none at all.

La Paz

BOLIVIA

AYORE
TRIBE

8

AYORE TRIBE

BOLIVIA

In 1942 New Tribes Mission made its first contact with the Ayore tribe in the southeastern lowlands of Bolivia. The brief contact with the fierce, nomadic tribe resulted in the death of those first five missionary men. It only served to reinforce the reputation the warring tribe had gained over the years that, being ruthless murderers, they deserved only to be hunted down and killed. But efforts continued by the missionaries, finally resulting in a peaceful contact a number of years later. The group was eventually settled in a place called Tobite, and the first of nine mutually hostile segments of the nomadic tribe was brought under the sound of the gospel message.

In the following years, linguistic work and cultural analysis were done, which sped up the peaceful contacts with the remaining groups of Ayore people. The tribe that today numbers approximately three thousand formerly wandered over an area roughly six hundred by four hundred kilometers (375 by 250 miles). As the distinct groups were contacted, they were settled in individual camps, each camp containing from two hundred to four hundred Ayore Indians. New Tribes Mission works in two of the five camps in Bolivia, and in one of the two in Paraguay. The others are ministered to by the South American mission, the Baptist Mission, and the Roman Catholics.

First and foremost of the work in the camps has been the establishment of New Testament churches, which has necessitated Bible translation, literacy programs, and discipleship classes. Much effort is also spent in the development of an economic program that enables the people to earn a living in a civilized world. It involves teaching them to make permanent houses, to practice new hygiene habits, and to expand their small farms into sizes that will produce a cash crop, enabling them to purchase staples such as rice, sugar, flour, and oil.

Over the past thirty-five years, since the first group was contacted, exciting progress has been made in each of those two areas. In the spiritual area, as more and more of the Word of God has been translated, the church has grown strong and daily continues to mature and evidence the fruit of the Spirit of God. Adult literacy programs and schools for the children have maintained high interest and motivation, resulting in a comparatively high literacy rate. Twice each year a conference is held in one of the Ayore camps. It is fast becoming the highlight of the year, as believers relate what God has taught them over the past months. It is always very stimulating to the host camp. On the physical front, the appearance of bicycles, radios, tape recorders, and new clothes among the Ayore people is evidence of a flourishing economy.

Twice in the past couple of years groups of Ayore men, believers whose hearts the Lord has challenged to preach the gospel to every creature, have endangered their lives moving out and contacting previously unreached groups of their own people. On their first missionary thrust, those Ayore missionaries reached twenty-five people, who were brought to Puesto Paz to be taught the Word of God. On the second, they reached a segment of the feared Pig People group of Ayore. Certainly the Ayore church is alive and well on planet Earth.

Along with teaching the Ayores about God, missionaries are helping them learn to produce cash crops to help purchase necessities.

"We learned what things to fear from out parents; if they were really afraid of something, then we were afraid of it too."

AJEI ETACORE

We learned what things to fear from our parents; if they were really afraid of something, then we were afraid of it too. They feared the bird [a nocturnal nighthawk] and we also feared it. We were without real understanding, that's why.

Our parents feared the Strange-light clan of Ayore people and fought with them regarding land and water rights. That was before I was grown up. They lived in great fear of one another. They'd go to the salt flats to collect salt every year, then they'd run from there as fast as they could.

The men didn't really want to go, but their wives sent them for the salt. We lived a long way from the salt flats, and we knew it was in our enemies' land. We also knew that they went to gather salt at that time too.

Our parents were really afraid; they feared war and fighting if they encountered their enemy. If the men had a lot of confidence in one of their group, they would leave him [as their protector] in the woods while they went out to gather salt on the salt flats. He was their believed-in-one; he would protect them from danger.

That is just as God's Word teaches—we have One in whom we trust and call Him our Savior, just as we called the one we left back in the woods to protect us. Our Believed-in-one protects us from wickedness and evil, too.

If someone we didn't know would come to our camp [when we were kids] we'd be afraid; even if he was one of our people, we were scared. We knew that fighting and war were always at hand, that's why. We were just kids and didn't know whether the newcomers were of our group or not. We'd run into the jungles and our mothers would look for us and bring us out. The arriving ones wouldn't kill us because they were of our family group. But, we never knew when fighting would break out.

Our fathers were fierce fighters. Only if they were really outnumbered did their enemies kill them. The Ayore warriors didn't kill women.

Our fathers believed in witchcraft. If someone had killed other Ayores, or was very wise, or was an old man, he could perform witchcraft. Then our believed-in-one healed us. We didn't really know the real Healer yet, that's why.

We had food enough if we could find it. The women would collect wild-pineapple-plant heart, or the boys would hunt turtles and honey. The men would find animals to hunt sometimes.

We'd come across dry desert areas when it was very dry, or a drought was hitting the area during certain times. We'd watch our fathers looking for water in dry riverbeds or in old swamps. If we'd find some water we'd stay there until it was gone. Then we'd look for water again and usually it was a long way off. Sometimes we had to go into enemy land to find water and food.

The men would say, "OK, let's go." We'd go as far south as the Paraguay border. We didn't dare go any farther as it was too dangerous. That was Pig People territory.

About twenty-five years ago Uejai [Ajei's people's main chief] went down to the Pig People country and warred with them. Uejai didn't dare go any farther south because there were a lot of civilized people down there. Uejai took over most of that territory in Paraguay, forcing the Pig People into a small area. Uejai was looking for better hunting and water sources for his people.

The Pig People didn't go up to the salt flats in Bolivia. It's said that they would eat a certain kind of dirt that tasted salty. They grind up lumps of dirt and then use it like salt.

The group of Ayore that live on the eastern borders of Bolivia and Brazil killed one of our witch doctors with their spears. Our people feared those witch doctors. With their powers they could bite and suck out the sickness of the sick people; they would really heal them; Satan's power was strong in them. They would drink tobacco juice and smoke their pipes, swallowing the smoke, and in that way receive power—they would fall into a trance then.

The people wanted to kill the evil witch doctor that was killed by the eastern group, but they feared him too much; he was very powerful. He woud try to kill his own chiefs, so his own people wanted to kill him. He finally went to the eastern group and they killed him there.

Our people still feared his power, even after he was dead—they believe that those powerful men can reincarnate themselves in the form of a tiger or whirlwind and seek revenge on their murderers or enemies.

When I was still a boy we had our first contact with some civilized Ayores at the salt flats. These civilized Ayores [with Bill Pencil of the South American Mission] were with us for awhile. Then we left for the woods again.

I was a teenager when Herschel Dunn reached us. Up to that time we still finished ourselves off on [gave ourselves to] our forefathers' beliefs. Others of our group came out to the civilized people before I did.

[Now] these days aren't like those days at all. We no longer fear war and killing and no longer lack water as we did so many times in the woods.

IQUEDE ETACORE

I no longer fear the things I used to; I now know real peace. It's not like it used to be in the woods before.

We used to be fearful of animals and taboos. We used to fear storms. We didn't live in houses, but out in the open. We feared the forefathers' spirits, which would come by means of lightning. The lightning did strike some people; they looked like a fire had burned them up. That's why we feared the lightning.

But I know that fear's origin is Satan—the devil sends fear. God keeps us from fear. Lightning hit a woman who was gathering food; it knocked her down; then she felt real cold all over. It really split her gallbladder [scared her]. When she got back to camp she fainted. The witch doctor worked on her, using the ways of the frog [particular type of witchcraft], and then she got better—he healed her.

We had great fear of things—the fear was of Satan. But these days we know we are God's possessions. He protects us and now we are not fearful. Fear of snakes and tigers no longer rules us.

I remember one night, a long time ago, when I was sleeping in the middle of the road. I was sleeping and heard a terrible noise that awakened me. I was all alone. The one who woke me up was over there. It must have been the middle of the night. I was really snoring— *co, co, co, co*—it was a tiger that woke me up and leaped out onto the edge of the road, coming toward me. I grabbed my lance, which was beside me. I saw it standing there, looking at me. If I hadn't awakened it really would have killed me. I was all alone. The others were far off.

I talked to the tiger, saying, "What do you want? Here I am if it's me you're after." It began walking down the road, away from me, then. I didn't dare move or it would have leaped on me.

Tigers are that way—they're very wicked—mean. This one wasn't real bad because it walked away from me. It walked off into the woods.

I kept my lance close by after that, in case it would attack me again. It was a good, long lance, with a sharp metal point. I was ready to kill it if it came back.

I had some narrow escapes, but God kept me from death. That's why now, even though I'm just one [alone] I'm not afraid; God protects me. We're God's possessions—that's why.

I'm not afraid of snakes either. I know God closes their mouths and keeps them from biting me. My insides always go to Luke 10:19, where it says that if someone believes in Me he can step on snakes and they won't bite. My insides never leave that promise of God. It says that scorpions won't bite us either. God loves us as we go along to various places—that's why.

TAMIDATE JUNMINORE

Enemy warriors killed my husband a long time ago. Everyone was sleeping soundly, lying on the ground sleeping. I wasn't sleeping. Their victim, my husband, lay there beside me. It was then that the enemy warriors attacked us.

During that battle they slashed my brothers' neck open along its side. He wasn't quite able to make it to the camp because of his wound. My husband chased them for a way, then he heard the yell that one of their men had been injured. As he turned to see who it was that was injured, the enemy speared him through the chest.

Neither of the two injured died right away. We cared for them all that day, but they died the next day. We cried for their nearness [mourned for them] all day and night. We knelt in the dirt, crying; we couldn't sleep. In vain we tried to keep them alive.

Just before he died [my husband] was crazily calling out the names of things. One of the other men told me to go outside the shelter, so he might not hurt me in his crazy state. I went outside, and soon they said, "He's now no more." [He's dead now.] It was a whole day and a little bit since he was wounded. I really missed my husband and cried for his nearness.

I had two little children by him. After my husband was killed the men killed my little boy [the custom when dependents are left after the death of parents]. My little girl stayed with me.

After that one of the other teenage boys wanted to marry me, but he already had a wife, so I ran from him. He kept following me, and finally I got tired of his advances. I followed him to the camp and became his wife. We had two boys.

Later he went crazy and walked off into the woods. He just suddenly went crazy. He'd call out the names of different things; he'd cry and was really afraid of fellow Ayores. Crazy people really feared the others a long time ago. He kept saying to me, "Bury me and then we'll go; they are going to kill us, that's why." But I didn't want to follow him. I kept telling him I'd blow on him [witchcraft] and on his eyes to make him better, but he said, "Forget it; don't," and kept himself from me. He told his kids to go with him—that if they didn't, the people would kill them. They cried, "Mommy, let's go, too." He packed his bag with his rope and his gourd. He put all of his boys' things in, too. Then he left.

The civilized people killed a lot of our people, but I wasn't with them;

I just heard about it. Some of the ladies didn't want to go gathering food where they went, because it was too close to the civilized people's village, but some went anyway. Some civilized men saw them and started chasing them on their horses. It was a grassland, and the horses could run fast.

They shot them down in the grass. Some of the young girls hid in the tall grass [she names five people that were killed that day]. They killed a man, and when they heard his wife calling for him, as she cried for his nearness, they rode over and shot her. They shot another man in the chest—*bang!* He fell down, with his bag falling over the top of him.

The bats chattered a lot at night, and they warned us if the enemy was near. Whenever we heard the bats chattering a lot, we were really afraid. We'd say, "Everyone be quiet; the bats are talking." We certainly were afraid of the civilized people.

The ladies were filled with fear of many things: various plants, deer manure, ant manure, fire ashes, anteater tails, animal hearts. If the kids took the lids off the cooking kettles, their hands would be eaten off by wildcats. They were afraid of twins and would bury them alive at birth—they were cursed, that's why.

Now during the days when fear wants to fill me, I pray to God and He gives peace. Also, when others falsely accuse me or are mad at me, I don't argue back or hate them; I just pray for them. I'm now not afraid of them or of their words. I used to be, but now I'm not anymore. It's OK if they kill me—I'll just go to heaven. I keep quiet.

We have water and food, also clothes. We don't fear the "bird." Our fears of the past are now for nothing.

9

YUQUI TRIBE

BOLIVIA

Bolivian colonists talked about the light-skinned Indians that roamed in their area of Bolivia. The colonists were from the high-altitude area of Bolivia—people who had come to carve homes and farms out of the jungle area. It was from those colonists that we first heard of the Yuqui Indians. In the 1950s, the wife of one of the colonists was at the river with her children washing clothes when an arrow from across the small river pierced her body. Her children saw her die before them on the river bank.

In revenge, the colonists asked the military to go in. They found a village with many of the men gone hunting. They killed some twenty Indians and took five children captive. The Indians retaliated by ambushing the colonists as they traveled alone in the jungle to and from their farms.

The people asked the New Tribes Mission to come in and pacify the Indians—an interesting time to enter into that picture! The situation became so bad that the colonists abandoned their homes and returned to the highland area of Bolivia. We continued our efforts to effect a friendly contact with the Yuquis. I remember my first encounter with them. The missionaries who were working on their contact sent an SOS to Cochabamba where we were living. Another missionary and I went down to the area to help. We traveled by boat from the little village of Todos Santos and finally walked several hours through the jungle, arriving at night at the clearing where the missionaries had made their headquarters. The next morning I was introduced to the Yuqui.

A week or so before, they had followed one of the trails out of the jungle into the missionaries' clearing to take the gifts that had been left for them. That is what we wanted them to do, but we had hoped that they would be friendly and willing to accept our gifts as tokens of friendship. They grew bolder and bolder until by their frequent attempts to choke us and the fear on the part of Bolivian nationals that we would bring the Indians out to where they were living, we felt that we should abandon that contact area and approach from another site. A houseboat was built and contact efforts were begun in another area still within the area roamed by the Yuqui people.

Now several years later, the missionaries are living in houses close to the Indian village. It is thrilling to see those Yuqui Indians who have been saved and to know that soon a translation of the New Testament will be in the hands of the Yuqui—work on the translation is well advanced.

IAQUIAINA

A long time ago I was really sad; I was sad for a long time. I was worried about myself, and when finding Jesus Christ I stopped worrying about myself. That's not how I was a long time ago; I used to be very afraid.

A long time ago, when I was young and my legs were very sore [a condition they feared was fatal and for which the treatment was bloodletting, carried out with a squirrel tooth] I was very unhappy about myself.

When I was sick I said, "There's no one to talk with [or pray to] about himself [oneself]." But I was wrong; I don't say that anymore. Since I believe in Jesus Christ I don't hesitate to tell about myself [pray] to God. Also, I wanted to talk to my dead grandfather's spirit. Since I regard God, I don't do that anymore.

A long time ago I used to be very afraid of my corpse [afraid to die]. Now I'm not. My husband also was one who talked a lot to the wind [spirits of the dead]. He was very reluctant to die. He didn't want to die and used to be so worried about himself.

My husband used to talk a lot to his dead mother, but then he desired to become a child of God. He really wanted to regard Jesus Christ. He formerly wasn't like that. When he disregarded Jesus he wasn't able to be even a little bit happy. That's how I was also a long time ago, when I didn't regard Jesus, when I was ignorant of Jesus and worried about myself.

I was very fearful that something would kill me—a spirit or snake. Since I've believed in Jesus I desire to be made happy by God. I had realized that I wanted to be bad, like I shouldn't be for God [as a believer]. Then I thought a lot about God, in order to have Him help me to understand. I admitted to God that I had been bad, then God said to me, "If you don't behave, the people are going to imitate you by also being wicked. Do you really want to regard Jesus?" "Yes," I said, "but why am I bad like I don't want to be? Why do I listen to Satan? Make me strong," I said to God. "Cause me to be able to resist Satan," I told God. "It's because you're able to be bad as well as good," God said to me. "Really think about me; my children can't just regard Jesus and do nothing more; they can't keep on being bad. It's because you've been wicked that you're sad. Tell all about yourself completely to me [confess]. When you tell about yourself I will forgive you," God said to me.

Then I told God all about myself; I told Him about everything, even my feet, that caused me to want to be disobedient. I told God to keep me from going around to get things I shouldn't. "You cause me to refuse the men who make advances at me; let me really think a lot about You, in order to be one that You make strong," I said to God.

Then God said to me, "You must truly regard Jesus Christ and My Breath [Holy Spirit] in order to be strong, then I will really be able to teach you well; then you will not just listen to my Word and not obey it. Really listen to me," God said.

That's why, upon hearing God, I was really very happy. I wasn't like that in the past when I was bad. I used to be very sad. I was even mad at the men also. "Why do the men keep coming over to see me, as they shouldn't?" I said to myself. "Why do I refuse them and then give in? Why am I wanting to be bad, like I shouldn't be, for God?" God told me, "If you aren't able to contain yourself [toward the men], you'll have to die."

Then I said to God, "Cause me to refuse the men." And God made me happy with Himself. I told God that it was because I was thinking wickedly like I shouldn't. That's why God caused me to not want to think about such things. It's because God is very strong; that's why He caused me to desire to think right and to think about Him and about Jesus.

I said to God, "Don't let Jesus' blood stop cleansing me." Also I told Him, "Alone, I'm not able to be good; You must make me good." Then I told God, "You must cause me to regard the people that I have been unkind to." After that God talked to me about the people, the ones I had disregarded. God told me that I wasn't just being unkind to people but also to Jesus when I was like that. I admitted that I had been bad to them and shouldn't have been. God told me not to listen to Him in vain; so I didn't forget what God told me—I told Him all about myself; I didn't tell Him about other people [their sins], just about myself.

I talked to my husband also—"You and I have been talking wickedly and making God sad," I said to my husband. "Jesus doesn't do like that, neither does God. Let's you and I cause ourselves to be made strong by God; let's hate our old eyes completely, since we've taken Jesus' eyes. The devil doesn't feed us—I don't want to be one who doesn't respond to God, because God doesn't reject us when we go to Him. God wants to make the slaves His children also [Iaquiaina's husband was a slave], in order to be ones He regards," I said to my husband. I also told my husband that when one of the slaves regards Jesus, he will be higher-class than his master who doesn't regard Jesus.

That's when my husband, not like previously, wanted to regard Jesus. My son, Little Squirrel, told his father, "Jesus is much better than you; why aren't you good, so that you can teach me to be good also?" Then my husband said, "May God cause me to understand so that I can be as I should for you." "You should really mean that," said Little Squirrel to his father.

Then my husband said, "God wants to make me understand now; God wants me to behave. I'm not able by myself to be good. Jesus, on the other hand, is much better than we are; I can't make myself good." That's what my husband said, talking about himself to us. Now my husband makes himself happy at night, telling God about himself.

Some of the people call my husband "the child of a slave," but my husband says, "I really hope that I can please God; I hope the people can see that I'm living right for the Lord." That's not what he said in the past. He used to be very disobedient. He used to always stretch out his hand [continually stole things]. He doesn't do like that since God talked to him.

It was when my husband slapped me in the face, that God said to him, "Why are you so abusive? Kiss your wife! Light the fire to warm her. Why are you so wicked to your wife? I'm going to show you your wickedness." God told him that if he kept being that way, disregarding God, that he would be one that would go to the fire when he died. Then my husband confessed to God; that's when my husband no longer ignored God. He came right over and kissed me.

Then I told my husband, "Let's be good for God; the one inside of us [Jesus] is able to be good; He's much better than you and I." I told him, "Those who are not on God's trail [unbelievers] have to go to the fire." Now my husband was no longer angry with me.

I used to be like my husband when I didn't regard Jesus, disobeying my mother. Then God said to me, "If one regards Me he will be able to grow upright and behave for his mother."

God said, "Let my children pray about each other to Me, and I will answer. If one teaches his relatives, telling them My Word, then I won't have children in vain from among the people. Would that many of the people might regard Jesus," He said. That's why I want to cause my relatives to be God's children. I desire that my relatives, when they see me living for God, do the same thing. Now I understand that it's Jesus who protects us from the fire.

In the past we were afraid of thunder; we thought it would kill us and were afraid of the storm. We used to be afraid of the little green bird also—and the red bird. We were very afraid of the nationals, too, in the past. When the people used to hide from the nationals, they couldn't let their babies cry; they would give their babies the breast quickly, so they didn't cry.

The people covered up their trails with leaves so that nationals wouldn't follow them. Now we have made friends with the nationals; we are not afraid of them anymore. Because of our fear of the nationals, we used to want to shoot them, but now that we have been taught, we aren't cruel to them anymore.

We used to be afraid of the spirits of dead people, too. When we heard the thunder we mistakenly thought it was one of our dead one's spirits, and we used to cry. Now the people listen to the storm and don't do like that any longer. They used to be afraid of the wind when it blew strongly; now we are not afraid of the wind anymore. We used to think it was our dead relatives' spirits that were charging at us in the wind, so we chanted at the storm and wind to make them stop. We thought [mistakenly] that when the spirits heard our crying they would stop.

We don't imitate our relatives from the past anymore, since we have regarded Jesus. God revealed His Son to us, and He showed us the fire [of hell] in our dreams. God said, "This is how it will be with the ones who do not believe in Me; they will go to the fire. You should regard Me." That's when I really wanted to regard Jesus.

It was at that time that I said, "I hope that I too will see God. Since God is good, I hope He will regard me, too." It's just been recently that we believed in Jesus. We used to not do so and were afraid of dead people's spirits when we were sick. We were afraid to die when we were sick. Now we aren't like that; it's because God has made us brave in Him.

Now I like to think about God and want to walk on God's trail. In the past we were very fearful. We were afraid of the rain right after someone had died. After the corpse's flesh had rotted off we were a little braver, but right after somebody died we were afraid of the rain, believing it could kill us.

The people were afraid of their slaves, too, after they died; they were afraid that their dead slaves' spirits would shoot them—that's because they believed that their slaves became strangers to them after they died and didn't recognize them anymore.

The people used to talk a lot to the red bird, too. "Watch out for me; don't let a snake bite me while I'm out hunting," the people said to their dead relatives' spirits, talking to the little red bird. Now the people don't talk anymore to the little red bird nor to the little green bird. They used to talk to them a lot.

The people used to plead with the spirits in the storm—"Don't let anyone fall on me [don't let the lightning strike me]—keep me alive" [let me live]. The people asked the dead people's spirits [through the little red bird] to cause them to shoot game.

Because we now regard Jesus, we don't talk to the birds anymore; we don't talk to the spirits in the wind or storm either. We now know that our relatives from the past didn't tell us the truth. Now we know that the spirits of the dead people can't hear us.

Our relatives from the past weren't like we are now; they were afraid of eating certain kinds of animals when they had a baby. They believed that a raccoon would kill you if you ate it right after having a baby. Now we are not afraid of that.

In the past, when someone's wife died, a man wanted to kill someone else right away to go along with her spirit. Now we don't kill each other. We used to kill the slaves too when their masters died, so they could accompany their masters' spirits. Now that we regard Jesus, we don't do that. We aren't cruel to each other anymore. In the past, when we didn't know God we used to turn our words over badly [we had bad thoughts]. But now that we regard Jesus, God causes us to turn our words over well for Him.

A long time ago, when the people would see their relative's corpse, they would stab themselves with bamboo-tipped arrows. Their friends would have to take their arrows from them so they wouldn't stab themselves.

The people used to get weak-kneed from hunger when someone died. They weren't able to eat for many days when someone died (this was to show the dead spirit, which was still around watching them, that they were really mourning for him). If he saw them eating right after he died, he could cause sickness or death; so that's why they fasted after a death.

However, the spirit couldn't see in the dark, so they used to sneak a little food at night. It was quite a revelation to them to find out that God can see as well in the dark as in the light.

They used to cry and wail until their throats got parched and sore; they cried till they were hoarse. They wanted to die along with the one they were mourning. Now that we regard God, He causes us to be able to eat. He causes us to be happy again. We used to think only about the dead relatives. Now we don't think just about ourselves and get sad.

The people used to have a lot of eyes [there were a lot of them], but they killed each other. That's why now we haven't made ourselves a lot of eyes. Since we have regarded Jesus, we have stopped killing one another. That's because now we are God's children.

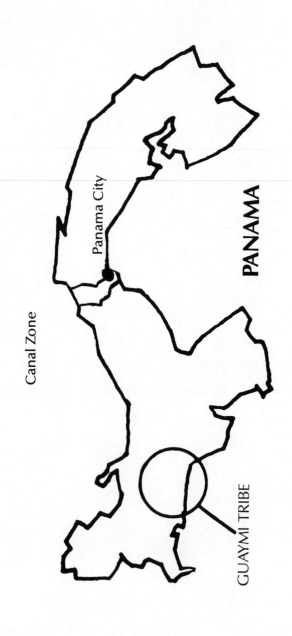

Canal Zone

Panama City

PANAMA

GUAYMI TRIBE

10

GUAYMI TRIBE

PANAMA

The western part of Panama is divided by a mountain range inhabited by the Guaymi Indians, a tribe numbering more than thirty thousand. Their contact with the outside world dates back to the time of Columbus. From those first encounters to the present, the Guaymis have become a civilized and law-abiding people.

By and large, their livelihood consists of farming rugged, mountainous territory. But the land is poor, overcrowded, and seldom produces enough food for the whole year. They live and work together in family groups. In some areas several families have built their thatched-roof houses close together to form small communities. Many of the communities now have schools and one or two small stores. Money for clothes, tools, and household goods is obtained by working a few weeks each year for the Latins.

Guaymis dress very modestly. Men generally wear shirts, pants, and either rubber boots or no shoes at all. The women wear the colorful full-length dress called an *inagua*. Men become skilled in the art of using a machete for everything from clearing brush to peeling an orange. The women keep the family fed by boiling almost everything they eat in a large metal pot over an open wood fire. Today most older children spend half a day at school and half at home doing chores such as carrying water, looking for firewood, or caring for younger children.

For the Guaymis, the battle for survival is not only against the natural elements of their environment, but also against the spiritual forces of evil. From childhood they are taught to protect themselves from evils such as accidents, sickness, and death that can come upon one through witchcraft and evil spirits. Often it becomes a very sad and fearful struggle. But in the areas where the gospel of Jesus Christ has been received, there have been many freed from enslaving fear.

In many ways, to live among the Guaymis is a step back in history—to a time when to live meant a personal struggle between man and nature, a way of life that would be considered hard and unbearable by some, but for the Guaymis is all they have ever known.

For the Guaymis, the battle for survival is not only against the natural elements of their environment, but also against the spiritual forces of evil.

VICTOR CORTEZ

My name is Victor Cortez. I was an orphan, raised by my grandmother. As a boy, I used to watch the sun and wonder who had made it. I also wanted to know why people died; and after they died, where did they go? There was no one to tell me these things, and I was often afraid of the unknown.

When I was still a young boy I was taken to the drinking and fighting parties that my people have each year. I learned that a "real man" was one that could drink much and fight hard. Soon I, too, was drinking and fighting.

One day my older brother left home to look for work in a Latin town. While he was there he met missionaries that had come to tell my people about Jesus. It was my brother that brought the first missionary to where we lived; her name was Eleanor Larson, and she told us about God.

After her visit she left, but my brother stayed and explained more of what he had learned from the missionaries. He told me that it was God who had made the sun and the earth. To me those words were like a drink of water when you are very thirsty.

I was interested in all the Bible said. I began to go where the missionaries lived, to hear more about God and the Bible. Many thought I was a believer, and I was even baptized, but I didn't fully understand yet. By that time I had married a young Christian girl. It was not long before I did come to know Jesus as my Savior.

I wanted to live for the Lord, but I also enjoyed drinking and fighting with unbelieving friends. I tried to tell my family that they too should obey the Lord, but they wouldn't listen because of the bad way I was living. My wife and I were not happy together because my life was filled with fighting and drinking.

Finally we left our people, and I got a job in a Latin town far away. For six years I worked in a brewery, and my drinking problem got worse. During those years we went to a Baptist church, but I continued to live the same old way. After those six years we returned to our people.

This time we lived in the area my wife was from. It was a small town, so I worked in town while my family lived in the mountains. At that time I decided to take a second wife. When I took my second wife home, my first wife became very angry. I had to threaten to leave her and the children, to get her to agree to let the other woman stay. Soon I had two women mad at me. I felt very bad about my sin. At the end of five months of living with two wives, I told the second wife to go away; that night she left.

But I continued my drinking and fighting. Sometimes I would come home and talk mean and ugly to my wife. I would get mad at her for talking to me about returning to the Lord. At times I would wake up after a drunken fight and be sad, and pain would enter my heart, even to the point of wanting to run away; but, where could I go? That made me very angry.

I knew that I should obey God. God's Word said that I needed to repent of my sin. Brother Bruce [a missionary] had told me that I needed to repent of my sin and come back to the Lord. My wife had also told me that my family was suffering greatly because of my life.

Finally I realized that it was true. It caused me to humble myself before the Lord. Then I confessed my sin to the Lord. Now I felt free, content, and happy. Soon after I had returned to the Lord, my oldest son was reading the Bible to me; he was reading Romans 8:1, "There is therefore now no condemnation to them which are in Christ." That truth entered my heart, and I began to cry and give thanks to the Lord.

It has been five years since the Lord changed me. Things are not like they were before. Now we have hope and peace; and if we have to suffer hardships, we have God's Word to encourage us.

I am very thankful for all the Lord has done for me. I often think of the verse where Jesus says, "Take my yoke upon you" [Matthew 11:29]. For me it means that I am to walk with the Lord and not go to the right or left, but just keep trusting in Him. That is the way I want to live.

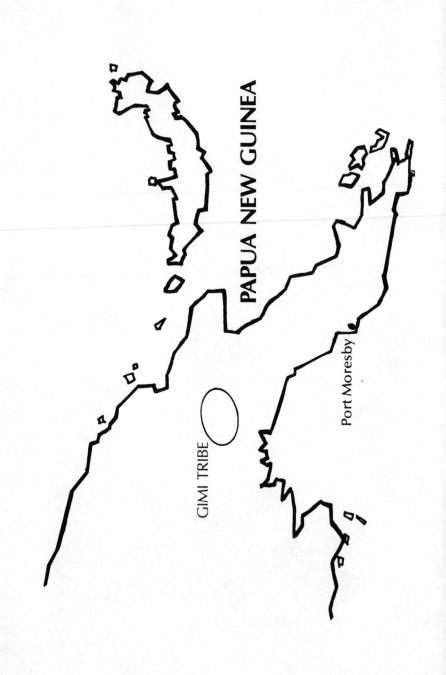

11

GIMI TRIBE

NEW GUINEA

The Gimi tribe lives in the eastern highlands of New Guinea, about seventy miles from the town of Goroka. They are situated behind Mount Michael, a peak with an elevation of over twelve thousand feet. South of them about three days' walk in the Papuan border. In September of 1975 Papua and New Guinea, formerly under British rule, united to form the independent Papua New Guinea.

Ten thousand people live in the Gimi valley, which is approximately twenty miles long by ten miles wide. They speak one of the seven hundred to eight hundred languages of the country. The short (average height is just over five feet) but muscular Gimis are subsistence farmers, spending a good deal of their time in the two or three gardens that each family has. Their staple food is sweet potato—coming in over thirty different varieties with new strains being brought in all the time. (A current new favorite is *sisi muni,* or "the sixth month.") They also plant and eat sweet corn, pumpkin, various greens, sugar cane, and sometimes potatoes. They raise pigs, but only kill and eat them on special occasions, such as weddings, feasts, initiations, when sickness strikes, or to make peace between enemy groups.

The Gimis believe that the earth is flat and that someone holds the edge of it. When the man gets hungry for sweet potato, he loosens his grip on the earth and it shakes—their explanation for an earth tremor! They say if that man ever dies, the whole earth will flip over.

They believe that when someone dies, he becomes a spirit, and they are especially afraid of the recent dead, believing that they come back to harass them. So the Gimi religion is nothing more than a series of ceremonies to keep those spirits "happy." For instance, if they go into a ground called *negi maa* and kill a bird or chop down a tree, they offend a spirit, and their sons are in danger. So they have to kill a pig or chicken and pour out the blood at the place of offense. Then the spirit is appeased.

The Gimis do not believe in natural death. Unless a very young child or older person dies, they believe that someone caused the death. Even if a person dies of sickness, they believe that someone is responsible. A person in our tribe recently died of dysentery, and the people still believed that someone else caused the death.

The Gimis claim that they have ways of finding out which group (not so much an individual) did the killing. Sometimes they cook possums and say the names of different groups. If the possum does not cook when they say the name of a certain group, they believe that particular group did the killing. Widows wear "Job's tears"—white beads made out of seeds—around their necks and heads and also put on rags, which traditionally they cannot take off until their husband's deaths have been avenged.

Some groups still keep that tradition, whereas other groups, who have had more exposure to the gospel, do not avenge the deaths in their group.

Dale Palmer of New Tribes Mission was the first missionary to go to the Gimi tribe in the 1950s. Progress was slow in those early days in some ways because, for instance, it took two or three years to build a horse road into the Gimi so that supplies could be taken in. In those days it took three days to walk from Goroka. But the Gimi people were overwhelming in their response to the gospel, and the early missionaries saw many coming to the Lord—big grass-roofed church buildings were built in the villages—and many folks eager to learn to read their own language.

No doubt their motives were mixed, but some of the converts from that time have stayed true, and some like Ireso are leaders now.

As we go into the eighties, we find the Gimi work still unfinished. The needs are basically in two areas: the church and the translation of the New Testament. New Tribes missionaries have started to have one- or two-week Bible conferences in the villages, when we study the Word and train leadership. We are praying that solid leadership will emerge from those conferences.

The translation of the New Testament is now sixty-five percent complete, and we are trusting that it will be in the printers' hands by 1982. We are looking to the Lord to do great things through us and for us, and to see our part of the Gimi work completed by, perhaps, the middle 1980s. We can then move on in the spirit of the apostle Paul, who said: "So have I strived to preach the gospel, not where Christ was named" (Romans 15:20). Then the work can be left to Ireso, Nana'oaba, and other faithful leaders that the Lord raises up.

NANA'OABA

Previously, when we lived in the old ways, we were involved in sorcery, fighting our enemies with bow and arrows, adultery, fornication, stealing and eating other people's pigs, telling lies sometimes and truth occasionally, and fighting each other; those were the things we were continually doing before.

When we took other men's wives, they shot us with bow and arrow, and we shot them back, a fight erupting. We had no way of settling that. We had no village courts in those days, so we killed a pig and gave it to them [those we had offended], and on top of that we also gave them shell money. And that's how we made things right, because there was no other way.

At that time we took part in singing (singing and dancing), weddings, and initiations. We were living like that when the bowmen [policemen] came. They came and started to court us when we stole other men's wives, or committed adultery, or stole and ate someone's pig. They courted us and made us give a big pig in exchange for what we had done. We also gave some shell money—that being the only way we could make it right, and there being no jail to which to send us.

We were still fighting with bow and arrow when those policemen came. They saw us fighting with the bow and arrow and told us it was a bad thing we were doing. "Be cool [make peace]," they told us. But we didn't listen, so they took our wooden shields and bows and arrows and broke and burned them in the fire.

Then they appointed some of our leaders as *luluais* [village government officials]. They also appointed *tultuls* to help them. They then started to conduct courts and send to jail those who committed adultery, those who stole, and those involved in sorcery. Those who became afraid stopped doing those things, but those who weren't afraid kept on doing them.

At that time I was committing adultery, stealing and eating other people's pigs, also stealing food. Then the missionaries came; they brought good ways with them and told us about the good ways. They told us which things were sin and that if we continued in them we would burn in the fires of hell. "Therefore," they said, "give liver to those things [regret or repent of them]."

And then they said: "There is only one road [to heaven] and we are going to show it to you—Jesus is the road." When they told us that, we wondered what kind of talk [message] it was, but after we prayed to God we saw it [realized, understood]. And having repented of [regretted] our bad ways [sins], we forsook them, saying "This is true talk, the truth." And we heard well God's talk [listened to it and embraced it]. We did that, and some of our ways left us and fled. We clearly saw that Jesus, our older brother, is the only road.

Having repented of my bad ways, I continually heard God's talk, the talk of my Father . . . and then I helped many men and women by teaching them God's Word. I showed them the Jesus Road and also baptized them.

I was continually doing that when I met a man named Ireso and taught him. Teaching him, he saw clearly [understood], and then he helped me to give out God's Word. Thus we two went on. When I fell, he got me up again, and when he fell I raised him up. That's what we have been doing and still are. That is a good thing. We are not to be lazy, but tell many men and women, "Here is the road; Jesus is the road."

IRESO

I want to tell you my story. Before I heard God's Word I didn't know that He had made the sun, the moon, and many things. I thought that many things (like killing people, bad talk, lying, thinking evil things) were good. But when Nana'oaba [see previous story] stood up [preached] and said that those were bad ways, I listened and turned around [was converted] and followed Jesus [became His disciple]—and I thought that Jesus was truly a good person.

I had thought that the moon, sun, and everything had come about on their own. And I didn't know from which road man had come—how man had come to be—but the missionaries came and told us: "God made the sun and moon, and He is the one giving us rain, and He is the one who made us. And when He says that everything must finish, it will, and the road for you to escape is not another, but Jesus only. Therefore, believe in Jesus and follow Him completely."

That is what they told us, and we put some of our bad ways [sins] behind our backs [forsook them] and came to Christ and were baptized. Also we taught many men and women, and some heard and were saved, but some didn't listen. We rejoiced about those who heard and were saved, but were sad about those who didn't listen. We were mad and also gave liver [felt compassion] for them.

Nana'oaba has already told you about how it was before the missionaries came and about how the missionaries showed us the road is a truly wonderful thing. It is a good thing that Jesus, our older brother, came down from heaven and died for us. But if the pink men [white missionaries] hadn't come and shown us the road of Jesus coming down and dying for us, we would have continually lived in the black thing [darkness], and our land and our bodies would have been no good [our whole way of life would have been no good], and we would have gone to burn in the fire.

But God, being a truly good person, sent the missionaries, and they came and showed us that Jesus is the road and He is the light. They did a truly wonderful thing in doing that. If we had been living still in the ways of our ancestors, we would all have been burning in the fire.

We really rejoiced when the missionaries came and told us that the road of escape [for when everything is finished] is Jesus. Before, when we lived in the ways of our ancestors, no one ever told us who made the sun or moon, or about Jesus' dying for us—but only the missionaries came and told us.

95

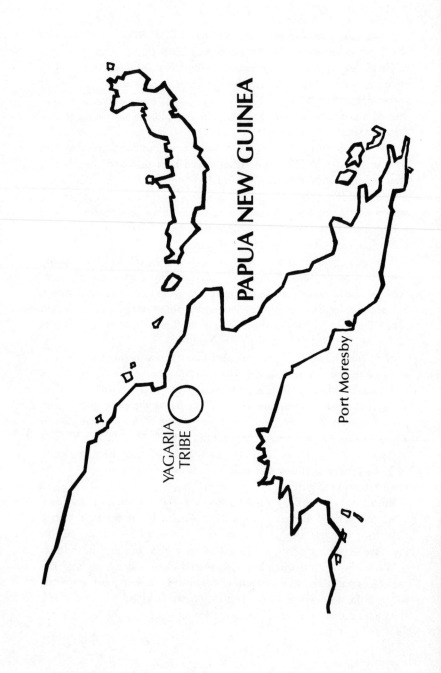

PAPUA NEW GUINEA

YAGARIA
TRIBE

Port Moresby

12

YAGARIA TRIBE

PAPUA NEW GUINEA

The Yagaria people (numbering about sixteen thousand) live in the eastern highlands province of Papua New Guinea, some twenty-five miles south of the town of Goroka. Most of them live in villages of fifty to two hundred people and, with the exception of a couple of hundred people (mostly young men) who are working in coastal towns, all live in that immediate area.

The terrain is quite rugged, and initial contact, before there were roads, was difficult. The government (Australian at that time) made the initial contact. Missionaries were then allowed to move in, in the early fifties. They were warmly welcomed for the most part, although it later became evident that much of their enthusiasm was a result of the hope for material gain.

Superstitions are many. Fear (mostly of sorcery and the spirits of the recently departed dead) governs much of the life of a Yagaria person before he or she becomes a Christian. Dwellings are usually small, round, windowless huts with grass roofs and dirt floors. Their diet consists of sweet potatoes for every meal of the day. They do have a lot of other vegetables, too, with which they supplement their diet occasionally. Meat is usually eaten only on special occasions such as birth celebrations, funerals, marriages, and initiations.

The Yagaria people live in a very rapidly changing society. Many of the older people well remember the days when they had never seen a white person, money, a car, or truck. They had never worn anything except their bark or homemade string skirts and had never eaten anything except that which they produced themselves.

Now, coffee crops are an adequate source of income. Papua New Guinea, whose independence from Australia was gained in 1975, now has her own currency. With the money received from the sale of coffee beans, the Yagarians purchase clothing, rice, cookies, sugar, canned meat, and fish from local stores. A few years ago, everyone walked everywhere, but now everyone, except a few village-bound elderly people, travels in community-owned trucks.

Although the living standard of most has been improved, contact with civilization has brought the evils of the white man, particularly drinking and gambling. Except for the several hundred Yagaria Christians, who have taken a stand against those things, the results have been disastrous.

The Yagaria live in a rapidly changing society. Older people remember the days when they had never seen a white person, money, or a car.

Lona Kanenu—"I believe it, and I'm thankful."

LONA KANENU

My name is Lona. Previously, when we were going to move [because of tribal wars], my husband would say, "Get going," and I'd take the bag of sweet potatoes and lead the pig. And he'd take the bow and arrows, and we'd go. We'd go to a certain place, and there they'd have war and kill the enemies. We were always doing that, moving around, having war. We were worshiping Satan then. But after one of our people had been killed, we'd feel very sad, thinking, "These are bad ways." And often we women would cut off a joint of a finger [in sorrow].

But then we heard that God gave Jesus to us as a free gift. Because of our sins, He gave Him to us. We heard that talk and put it into our stomachs [believed it].

Now I've heard that Jesus came down and died for us; that He had a lot of pain and shed His blood for me. And I believe it and I'm thankful. I'm so happy because He died and then went back up. Jesus' blood has cleansed my insides completely, and now I'm following Him. He took absolutely all of my sins and buried [removed] them completely. He died and rose again. I believe that.

Now that we've believed that Jesus died for our sins, we know that we'll be going to heaven to be where our Jesus is. In the afternoon, in the morning, and at nighttime I pray, "O, God, I know You're up there in heaven; You see us all the time; I worship You. Now I'm Your child, and I know that later I'm going to go up there to be with You."

That's how it is, and I've finished telling you.

Jonah learned to read about Jesus as a very old man. "I know that I'm already an in-heaven-person."

JONAH KOLOVEGU

My name is Jonah, and I'm going to tell you something. I'm Jonah, a person who was truly a very, very bad person and who used to always be at war. That's me—a man from a long time ago [very old]. I would have gone to hell for sure. But then the missionaries came and said to me, "Do you believe that Jesus came down from heaven and died for your sins?" And now I've decided to follow Jesus. I'm trusting Him, I'm rejoicing in Him and always praising Him. I mean that there's nothing at all on this earth that can help us at all.

I wasn't living in a good time before. It was a very bad time, with a lot of fighting, a lot of sin, all kinds of trouble. My older brothers, my younger brothers, my father, and my uncles were all killed by our enemies during the time of fighting. And I'd still be spending my life trying to kill the enemies who shot them. But the missionaries came and told me the gospel. Since I heard it and am a follower of Jesus, I've turned from all those old things, and they've gone far away.

I know that I'm already an in-heaven-person. I've gotten a completely new way of living since I believed. I've left my old way of life, and when people see me they say, "That's a man who used to live differently, but now he's gotten an entirely new way of life." They realize that I'm different, and that's what they say.

I was a warrior, and I used to get shells and salt for betraying and killing people. That was before we had money here; we just had shells and salt. But now there's money, and God provides money for us Christians so that we can buy clothes and food.

You sent word that you were going to make a book, so I'm telling you these things about how I used to be in tribal wars, always doing many bad things, living under Satan's control. I always slept in a bad place, I was always moving around, I was always out in the rain. My whole body, my feet, and everything were always wet, and I was always cold, living outside. My head was outside, too. But now that I've heard about Jesus and become a Christian, I live in a good house. I stay in a good place, not moving around to hide from the enemies, and everything is so much better for me.

Satan's people think, "There's no God; there's no Jesus." That's what they think, but now we've heard, we've seen, and we live in fellowship with Him, living in great joy. We're so thankful to God; we're so thankful to Jesus.

The talk about us Christians dying together with Jesus—I read about that in God's Book, the Bible. I'm really thrilled with that talk that I read in the Bible. But I'm not a man who had gone to school before, or anything like that.

I didn't have the Bible-Book before. I was just always walking around, fighting people, following Satan. But in order for us to find out and understand clearly about Jesus and about God, our missionaries translated the Bible into our language and said, "This is about Jesus. Read about Him here." They gave us God's Word in our language, so now, even though I'm a very old man, I'm so happy that I can read it, and that I'm going to heaven.

I want to tell you about my wife, too. My wife, Dale, was in the same kind of condition as I was before. She had been married three times, and all three men had been killed in tribal wars. Her husbands had other wives, too, and Dale was always fighting with the other women. She was really a fighting woman, but now, since we've both heard about Jesus and become Christians, and she's married to me, she's so different. She doesn't fight with people any more. She just lives peacefully.

The two of us really live well together, but we don't do that on our own. Oh, no. Rather, God says to us, "This is the way you should live," and we obey Him and live peacefully together. He has made us to live together in unity, and because Jesus' talk is true, now we live coolly [peacefully] together. I'm telling you that we're really happy. So later, if you want to see if it's a young man or an old man who told you this, you come and see the two of us here together, and you'll realize that this is the way it is.

AVIZA UTESO

You listen well to what I'm going to tell you. I'm a very old woman; my name is Aviza. I'm not originally from the Yagaria area, but I'm from a different place—the Koto grasslands area.

But this is what I'm going to tell you. When I was young, my mothers and fathers, my aunts and uncles, lived just like my grandparents and ancestors had. And I was there with them at Koto, and they traveled all around. They'd go from one village to another, all of the time having tribal wars, killing people. And I'd go with them, carrying my mother's string bag with the sweet potatoes for them.

It was like that, but then I came and came and came [a long way], fleeing from our enemies, and I came here to the place of the Yagaria people. I moved and was here in Yagaria land when the missionaries came. They came here, bringing God's Word.

When they told us about God, the others didn't believe it at first, but I thought right away, "I think that talk that they're telling us about God is true." And so I said to some of our young men, "You'd better go work for those missionaries who say that our Father, God, is in heaven, and listen well to what they have to say." So I sent them to work, and my son, James, too, went to work for the missionaries.

I was really sorry because I had done so many bad things, traveling around, helping them to carry their weapons and things like that, for the wars. So I wanted my son to listen to what the missionaries had to say and then to explain it to me.

My son was young then, but he worked [for them] and then he understood God's Word, and lifted it up [knew it was important]. He explained it to me and both of us believed that God sent Jesus, and that He came and died for our sins.

The two of us went all over to a lot of different villages, going, coming, going, coming [traveling around]. We told the gospel to people all over, and people from a lot of Yagaria villages listened to us.

At first they thought that we were just saying something we'd made up ourselves, but we said, "No, we're telling you God's talk." And we kept telling them about Jesus.

Now my son is grown up, and I've become a very old woman. And I want to tell you this: When Jesus came down and died, He died for my sins. I believe that, and so I tell the people from all the villages around. I tell them, and tell them, and tell them. I never stop thinking

105

about God's Word—when I get up, when I go to bed, all of the time. I'm always thinking about Jesus, following Him, and thinking about going to heaven.

I realize that I was a sinner, but I've left all that now and I'm following Jesus, that's all. And God knows when He's going to tell me to come up to heaven. When He says, "Come on up now," I'll go up.

Because I'm thinking about God and about Jesus all of the time, I don't think about things of this earth anymore. When they have tribal dances and feasts and things like that, I don't go. I stay home, and everyone realizes that I'm following Jesus. I'm always trusting Him very strongly, thinking, "My God lives." I, the one who's telling you this, am a person who's on the road that Jesus has opened for me.

But all people everywhere are sinners. When you hear what I'm telling you, you'll think that it's good that I've heard about Jesus and am talking about Him. We've heard the good news about Jesus, and we're on the road that He has opened for us. But some people haven't heard this. So you'd better think well about those people who haven't heard yet.

A long time ago my son James heard the gospel and believed it. And now he's working for the government. And the young men who are now in our Yagaria Bible School say to me, "Our mother, you helped to open the road for us to hear the gospel. It's the way that Jesus Himself opened, but you helped us by taking our ears [exhorting us], and now we've believed, too." They say that, but it's God Himself who is our helper, and who has opened up the road for us to go to heaven.

I believed first, and then I told my sons and my daughters and all my relatives, "I've come into God's fence, and I want you all to come, too. Come," I told them. I took their ears [exhorted them] like that, opening their ears for them [helping them to understand]. And now my sons and my daughters and my sons-in-law and my daughters-in-law are walking on God's road, too.

KOLOBUSA FEGELO

A long time ago, when I was small, this is what the adults used to say to me. "Look out," they said. "The spirits of the ancestors will shoot [harm] you. And the spirits that live in the forest will kill you and eat you, so be careful." They always talked like that to me, and I was always so afraid, just trembling in fear.

At that time, I was so fearful of a lot of things, but then when the missionaries came here, they brought God's Book and they told me like this from it: "Jesus came down to take care of all of those things that you are continually living in fear of," they said. "So believe in Him, become a new person, and live with Jesus."

After they told me that, I became a Christian. I became a a new person and rejoiced very, very much. And I'm still rejoicing very much.

Previously I always was living in great fear of all kinds of things. When I was small, the people were always having wars. When our fathers were getting ready to go to fight, they'd say this to us boys: "Listen; we're going to go and hide and watch for the enemies during the night. When it's light, your mothers will cook sweet potatoes and give them to you, and you take them to us." After they'd tell us that, they'd leave. So then in the morning, we'd take the food to them. We'd also take arrows that they had left behind. I'd go with the other boys, and we'd give our fathers their food.

They'd always go at night like that. They'd watch and watch and watch for the enemies to come. They'd watch until it got light. Then in the morning we'd take them the food, like I told you. They would eat it, and then when the sun came up and was shining brightly the enemies would appear. Our fathers would see them, and then the war would start.

As we were watching them, being so afraid, they would just keep on fighting. That's when I was small. I used to watch them fight and be so afraid. My fear—that's what I'm telling you about.

But now I'm so happy. If the missionaries wouldn't have come and told me about Jesus, I'd still have the same kind of stomach-ears [thoughts and emotions] as I did when I was young, and I'd still be living the same old way.

But when they came and told me about Jesus dying for my sins, I thought, "That talk is true," and I became a Christian. I'm so happy now. I'm so glad that I know that later Jesus is going to come again and take me to heaven, where I'll always live with a cool stomach [a heart at peace].

Now I'm not concerned about a lot of different kinds of things. I don't worry about anything at all; I just always think about Jesus. Because the truth is that Jesus came down and died for all my sins. With His blood, He paid for my sins, and He opened the road for me to go up to heaven, and because of that, when He comes back, He will take me to heaven.

Later when I go to be with Jesus, I'll never die; I'll live forever and forever, and be even happier!

What I'm telling you is absolutely the truth, about my rejoicing because of Jesus and about the fact that if the missionaries wouldn't have come, I'd still be living just like I was when I was young. But now my fear is gone; it's gone very far away from me, and I have peace and joy in Jesus. And every day I think about how I'll always live with Him.

If I wouldn't have heard about Him, later I'd have really gotten into severe trouble. I would have been lost. But it's true, that Jesus came and died for our sins. He opened the road for us to go to heaven. If we believe that, we become new people.

The news about Jesus coming back again to get us and to take us to heaven is really true, too. So I'm always rejoicing, as I wait for Him to come back and to get me to go to heaven to live. That's the end of the talk about my joy.

PARAGUAY

Asuncion

ACHE
TRIBE

13

ACHE TRIBE

PARAGUAY

The Aches are a tribal group living in the eastern part of Paraguay. They were for many years a nomadic people, greatly feared and considered to be "savage" by the other national people of Paraguay.

Roaming the jungles with their bows and arrows, they made their living from hunting wild animals and gathering fruits, honey, and other vegetation of the woods.

The Aches did not limit their hunting to wild animals nor their gathering to jungle vegetation. They found it a great challenge to kill cattle and horses belonging to the national country Paraguayans and frequently raided their gardens, specifically for corn and *mandioca,* a potatolike food. They could steal everything from the garden in one night (especially making good use of rainy days and nights) that the Paraguayan family had worked for all year.

Needless to say, the Ache people's stealing from the farmers caused a good many battles, but the Aches saw the civilized Paraguayans as intruders into their territory too. Many workers entered into the jungle to cut down the palm trees to get the palm heart (*palmito*), for which there is a big market. They were taking food that the Aches considered to be theirs. One can see the problem that existed for both parties. Meanwhile, neither trusted the other, and there was great fear on the part of all involved.

Because of those fears (and deaths of parties on both sides), attempts were made to make peaceful contacts with the Ache—for their own safety and because it truly was getting impossible to any longer "put off" meeting up with civilization. The days of existing off the jungle were coming to an end, and while they continued to steal for sufficient food, there would be no peace or safety for either party.

Many of the Aches had already made appearances on their own to the civilized peoples of the area for various reasons. Some had become sick with influenza and other diseases, and the Aches did not have the resistance to withstand illness. Because of the physical condition of the

111

people at that time and their inability to help themselves, New Tribes Mission workers (known already by the Paraguayan government to be interested in working with the people) were asked in 1972 to step in and help with the medical work on one of the government colonies for the Ache.

The Ache are lovable people, friendly and outgoing. We have made some very good friends among them. They are short in stature, oriental-looking through the eyes, very broad-chested (from pulling the bow), and very intelligent. We found them to be extraordinarily curious and interested in everything around them, and they learned new things quickly.

Anthropologists and others have opinions as to the origin of the Aches (some declaring they trace back to the Vikings), but no one has really come up with specific evidence to ascertain just where they originated. *Our* big concern, of course, is to help them where they are *today,* with a concern for their *future* and their *eternal destination.*

There are three dialectical groups of Ache, all mutually intelligible. Their skin color varies from rather dark to those with very white skin. (Dialectical group is not dictated by lightness or darkness of the skin.) Some of the Aches were at one time cannibals, and there was a time in the not-too-distant past when the other Ache groups were still very much afraid of the cannibalistic group. Most of those fears have been overcome today, and one will find Aches from all three groups willingly living together in one colony.

The entrance of the gospel has made a tremendous difference among the Ache people. They once lived in horrible fear that their dead relatives would come back in the form of evil spirits to kill them. They were afraid that the rainbow that they thought was a big snake would swallow them (they believed it wandered through the woods to get them when not up in the sky after a rain), that the falling stars were dead relatives coming back to burn them up, and that angry deceased relatives brought the storms. One can imagine how it thrills our hearts today to see them freed from so much superstition and fear.

They are happy as they are??? We have lived there. We have taken care of them when sick; we have seen them frightened through fear of the "unknown" and "invisible realities," and *we know better.* It is truly a joy to visit those people today and see the difference: joy and happiness in place of fear. Changed lives, indeed—and we are so grateful. So are they!

Today the Aches are also learning to do many things for themselves

112

that they previously did not have the knowledge to do. They are gardening sufficiently to sell crops to outside neighboring merchants. They handle a "store" of their own, making available other foods, clothing, and other items to their own people. They have taken an interest in building and have built a school as well as several personal houses. A large percentage of the younger Ache people are "literate" and looking forward to the day they can compete on an equal level scholastically with the national Paraguayan community. Many of the Aches are now registered with birth certificates and other legal documents, giving them proper Paraguayan citizenship rights—not a reality until very recent years. There is much to be completed yet in that area.

We give praise to God and to Him alone for the work that has been accomplished among the Ache people. There is still much to be done in discipling and Bible translation. We appreciate your prayers!

Aches once believed that the rainbow, a snake, would swallow them.

ANTONIA MERIEDA

Since hearing my brother Jesus Christ's Word, I'm no longer afraid at night. Before, I was afraid walking at night in the jungle. I was afraid of tigers. I was afraid sitting in the dark that an evil spirit might come. I was afraid!

I'm brave now that Jesus Christ gave me His Spirit. I was afraid in the woods. I didn't want to walk in the woods, perchance a snake would bite me. I was afraid of snakes! A snakebite hurts bad, therefore I was afraid.

Now I'm real brave. At night I was a "scaredy-cat," one who was afraid. My liver didn't exist at night. I didn't want to sleep. Now I sleep good. I was really afraid when evil spirits whistled. I didn't want to sleep when I saw evil spirits.

Before, we didn't love our husbands. Now, since hearing our brother Jesus Christ's Word, we really love our husbands. I'm real happy now; I'm real brave now, since hearing God's Word. When my husband went far away I was afraid. Now my husband works far away. When my husband works far away, I sleep alone. I am no longer afraid.

When my husband works far away I go to my foreign sister's house and wash clothes. I also cook and eat there. Then my brother Paul [Heckart, a missionary] says to me, "Are you really happy now?" I'm real happy. Paul says, "I'm happy, too."

From living with Paraguayans in Asuncion, I've come here in order to hear God's Word. God brought me here. I'm real happy here since hearing our brother Jesus Christ's Word. We're happy now.

Now I have a lot of sisters in the Lord. Now I don't talk bad anymore to my sisters. Now I love my sisters in the Lord.

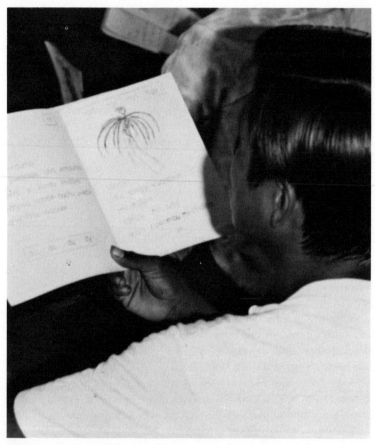

A large percentage of the younger Ache people are literate and are looking forward to the day they can compete scholastically with the national Paraguayan community.

FAUSTO GARCIA

Since hearing Jesus Christ's Word, we're no longer afraid. We used to be afraid when we heard evil spirits whistle. Now upon hearing our brother Jesus Christ's Word, we're no longer afraid like that. Now our bodies are good [we're content or satisfied] upon hearing [obeying] our brother Jesus Christ's Word. Upon God giving us His Spirit we've a "good body" now in exchange.

Our foreign brother came to tell us God's Word. Then it was through them we heard. Therefore, our bodies are good now [content or satisfied]. Therefore, we're no longer afraid of evil spirits; not anymore, since hearing our brother Jesus Christ's Word. Satan doesn't touch those who belong to our brother Jesus Christ.

Before, He didn't say that about us. Now He does. "Don't touch my children," He says.

Before, we were mean, too. We're not like that anymore. Now we have a new [body] in exchange because of our brother Jesus Christ. His Spirit entered our chests and is in our hearts. Therefore we now have good talk. Before we were really naughty. Now we're happy since hearing God's Word.

Before, we used to hit our wives. Now we obey God's Word. We're no longer afraid of evil spirits or Satan. We're not afraid of wild animals now, not even wild pigs. We were afraid, as kids, when we went into the woods. We were afraid for nothing; if a branch or something snapped or sounded, we were afraid a tiger might eat us. Tigers eat Aches. Now we won't be afraid of tigers anymore. Now we have our brother Jesus Christ's Spirit.

HIGENIO DUARTE

I am going to talk in Ache language. We'll talk to our brothers in Ache. You tell us in Paraguayan language, too. Then we tell our fathers. We tell our own people, even the grandmas.

Now we are healthy. There is no sickness [or death]. Before, we were not healthy. Then after you who belong to Jesus Christ came, we don't die anymore. Because of medicine we don't die. Now we eat food from the store, and we're healthy. We used to all have bad bodies [sickly]. And we used to be mean; all of us [Aches] were mean. Now since hearing [obeying] Jesus Christ's Word, we're no longer mean.

Before, we used to walk around at night. We were like dogs. We used to whistle around someone else's wife. Since hearing God's Word we no longer walk around at night. We tell all our brothers, "Don't walk around at night, those who belong to God. Evil spirits are those who walk at night."

Now those of us who took hold of Jesus Christ's hand, if our bodies hurt us we call to Jesus Christ, to our Father in heaven. Then we say, "Make our bodies good when we sleep, all our brothers, too." Then we say to our brothers, "If your body is weak, call to God; He takes good care of us. Don't be afraid to call. Tell all our brothers about God, too. Don't be afraid; for that reason God made mouths, to tell of Him.

He made ears, too, in order to hear. Some will go to other places to tell their brothers that God made eyes. There is no other creator; God made the whole world, the moon, sun, and fire. It was the evil one who didn't make anything. God is the one who made it all.

Paraguayans bow to idols for nothing. We're not like that. Paul, [Heckart] the missionary, isn't one either who lies or deceives like that. They [the missionaries] don't have idols like that. They [the missionaries] call to the one who is in heaven. This is what our brothers in Christ, who are here, say: "You bow in vain to idols; they don't heal."

Before, we used to drink liquor; now we no longer drink. One who drinks liquor is mean. Now we no longer drink, because that's really bad.

We were weak when we had the evil one. We were really afraid; we beat one another for nothing. We didn't like that. Then we said to Phillip [Phillip Mendosa, a Paraguayan believer], our Christian brother, "What? We're going to follow God? We're going to hold our brother

118

Jesus Christ's hand?" "Come," he said. We didn't any time [for some time]; then a lot of Aches hands were held. He said, "Why do you hold Jesus' hands?" "[Because] we don't want to go to hell; we want to go to God's place; it is said that we'll have good bodies there. It's said that where the evil one is there's suffering."

If the missionaries were not here, Antonia would have died. She had something big in her stomach; if it had burst, she would have died. We then called to God for her—"Make well our sister." We'd have cried if she had died. Antonia lives because of our brother Jesus Christ.

14

LENGUA TRIBE

PARAGUAY

The Lengua tribe of western Paraguay numbers about fifteen thousand. New Tribes Mission moved into the main village of the southern dia--lect group of those semicivilized people in 1952.

In the early 1900s, the people were still nomadic and quite treacherous. The few missionaries that lived in Paraguay at that time were threatened and came close to being poisoned by some of the more savage warriors. The tribe then began moving toward civilization, mixing Paraguayan culture with their own.

An English mission began working with the Lengua about 1920. Some of the missionaries really knew the Lord and others apparently did not. As a result of the formality imposed on the tribe, many professed to become Christians. It was quite evident that most of the new converts were not really born-again people, although they had learned to recite prayers, sing hymns, preach, and generally go through the motions of being Christians.

When most of the missionaries had abandoned the work and returned to their homeland, New Tribes Mission moved into the village.

Through the preaching of the gospel, several trusted Christ in January 1956. Makthlawaiya was the center of real Christian activity for years. Because several of those new converts wanted to be taught in God's Word, a discipling ministry was started.

The Indians then began witnessing to their people, and for years Indians were saved almost every week. Not only did those folk witness at home, but they traveled from village to village, telling of Christ and His love.

The missionary no longer lives with that tribe. The Lenguas have their own pastors, elders, and evangelists. They have the entire New Testament in their own language now. Hundreds of people have responded to the gospel, and the spiritual work continues among them in western Paraguay.

Elias Gomez–"God has chosen me to preach the good news among the Lenguas and other tribes."

ELIAS GOMEZ

I am a Lengua Indian; Elias Rufo Gomez is my name. I am an evangelist among the Lenguas, Sanapanas, Angaites, and Tobas.

I was born at Makthlawaiya, Mision Inglesa, in the *chaco* [dry flat grazing land] of Paraguay, on August 30, 1921. Eight days later my father and mother took me to the church building to be named and baptized, in order to be called a Christian.

I was raised in this place and went to school there. When I reached fourteen years of age I left school. Then they wanted me to read the Book at church on Sundays at the prayer meeting, and I read the Book before getting up. From 1946 I worked in the school as a teacher. While I was in school teaching I also preached the gospel. However, I was not a Christian; I did not really know Jesus Christ. Jesus had not changed my insides; I did not have new life.

I taught in the school and preached the gospel for a long time. I worked in the school thirteen years. During those thirteen years I did not know Jesus Christ in my insides, but I was called a Christian, though only in name, and in name I was also an evangelist.

I trusted in my infant baptism, and father's and mother's faith, and the bishop's laying his hands on me; but Jesus was not in my heart. I did not understand—I knew the name of Jesus, but I did not recognize [know] Him.

In the year 1953 we saw another evangelist who came into our midst; his name is Les Pederson. He preached the gospel very strongly. I listened to this message. During his message my insides worked; this message was right, I knew. I was not a Christian, and I pretended to be an evangelist. I was ashamed; my insides were ashamed because of my ways, being a liar.

Because my friends knew I was an evangelist and I preached before them, I didn't want to tell these unbelievers. My friends saw that I always had on a long robe at church on Sundays, as was the way of my church. Now I see Jesus; I know He is my Savior!

Then I left my church. Many of my people were angry because I left their church. My long robe died, my insides changed, and my ways changed—it was God who did it to me, it was God who changed me.

God has chosen me to preach the good news among the Lenguas and other tribes that are in the Paraguayan *chaco*.

This is my testimony so that you folks will know. Look at the way I was; I was without understanding. I really know the good news; I can preach it. But, are you an unbeliever? Trust Him with your heart.

MORO TRIBE

PARAGUAY

Asuncion

15

MORO TRIBE

PARAGUAY

Feared and respected by those living in their area the Ayores (also called *Moros* by outsiders) of the northwest *chaco* were legendary all across Paraguay as being vicious and cruel killers. Sudden and surprise attacks on remote farms, campers, or oil company employees often left several dead or dying from being clubbed on the skulls or from arrow and spear wounds. It made no difference whether the victims were men, women, or children. There was only hostility between them and the civilized population, with the exception of the Mennonite colony who tried to reach them with the gospel. The first Mennonite missionary was speared to death near an oil camp in 1955. Later, in 1962, a large group of Indians voluntarily came out of the woods and went to the Mennonites. They were turned over to the Roman Catholics because the Mennonites had no one to work with them. It was not until 1966 that another attempt was made, by New Tribes Mission that time, to reach the large group still in the jungle.

Under the leadership of a senior missionary, five people made a seven-day trip by horse and wagon the one hundred fifty miles into Moro territory. With the help of a semicivilized Moro by the name of Jose, who went along as an interpreter and go-between, and the perfect timing of our all-powerful God, a contact was made with a small group of Moros near Cerro Leon (Lion Mountain) in northern Paraguay. After the excitement of the meeting with the dark, nearly naked, pony-tailed warriors and the timid and distrustful women, a couple of days were spent gaining their confidence. An agreement was made to come back again in a month or so. Jose told the Moros that the missionaries wanted to live with them and teach them about God. They were also promised food, clothing, and axes in exchange for work.

From the start, the missionaries set up the policy of no handouts. All food and other essentials were given on a trade or work basis. Money was introduced as soon as possible. Skins and curios were marketed in order to help them get the clothes, food, tools, and shot guns and shells they wanted. Though they bullied and demanded at times, no compromise was made on that policy other than for medicine, which was given free. From the start they learned to work or trade for their needs.

Little progress was made on the language the first year and all spiritual work had to be done through the semicivilized Moros. It was hard work because of the distance from the source of supply. All supply work was still being done in part by horse and wagon. Bob and Helen Goddard, Norman and Linda Keefe, and their families lived there the first year. Because of Helen Goddard's health, Bob had to step out of the work and the Henry Bechegger family took their place on the team. The Bucheggers having worked with the Ayore people in Bolivia for years, already spoke the Ayore language. Under the teaching of Mrs. Buchegger, the Keefes also began to make more progress in the language. Henry Buchegger began teaching and preaching almost immediately after arriving. A few Moros expressed faith in Christ, but for several years the warriors still went out on raids against an enemy group they called the Pig People (another wild Ayore group) and showed little respect or concern for the men, women, or children they killed.

Because of drought and lack of permanent water at Cerro Leon the Indians moved in 1968 to a new location about ninety miles south. Here a permanent base was established with housing for the missionaries and Indians. A cattle program was started to help support the project, and work was continually made available to the Indians. Many of them still brought in tiger and ocelot skins to augment their earnings. That also helped develop the economic program and make many improvements. The gospel was continually taught and preached by Henry Buchegger and his wife, but even at the new place several raids were made on their enemies the Pig People, and more of them were killed. They still could not see how it could be wrong to kill their archenemies, whom they considered wicked and no good anyway.

Though there were some who believed the gospel and showed some fruit, there was no real break until 1976. Then Ayore preachers from Bolivia came down with some of the missionaries and preached and taught for a week. My, what excitement and what testimonies were given, as the gospel preached by other Ayores began to reap the harvest from the sowing of several years of missionary work! Over 80 percent of the tribe gave testimonies of salvation, many of them women, who had responded very little up until then. Others confessed their sins and expressed a new understanding of the gospel. They were literally set on fire. The smoking pipes, which were connected with their old life, were thrown away and for the first time many wanted to preach to their enemies instead of killing them. A strong desire to learn to read replaced the disinterest they previously had. Now they wanted to be able to read the portions of God's Word that came down for our translators in Bolivia.

Over the next few years they continued to grow in grace through the study of the Bible. More than twenty Ayore men preached and taught the Word. They became extremely responsible and trustworthy workers in all they did. They religiously saw that their debts were paid, sought work in the Mennonite colonies nearby, and proved themselves to be the best and most sought-after workers of all the tribes. Their industry won them the respect of the Mennonites, who had once feared their raids. They proved to be good managers of their money and gave of their means as unto the Lord, at times even giving small gifts to the missionaries. Now, with 7,000 acres of land given to them by some local Mennonites, they are all working together to buy a tractor on their own, to better farm the land the Lord has provided. They are putting the Lord first and hope to develop an economically sound colony that will honor the Lord.

ICADIGUEDE

Back in the old days, when we were in the jungle, we feared the coming of the month when Asojna, the bird, cried. Then they would say, "Look for water." (This was the dry season.) Then we looked for a waterhole. Then we camped by it in fear that we might not do what was required.

We waited for the first cry of the bird. When someone heard the cry we went into the woods. After we finished the ritual that the bird required they would say, "Now the jungle is good." Then the woods were really good for us. Before, the jungle was heavy and hard because of Asojna's curses.

We were also afraid of enemy groups that would come and kill us. But the bats and two other kinds of birds would call first, and we would know the enemy was coming. We were really afraid of those cries because then we knew we might be killed.

There were so many things in the jungle that we feared. The women were especially fearful. [Note: enemies killed women and children alike; there was no respect of persons.] The women feared battles, the civilized people, and so many things. Fear was with us all the time. It's like the Pig People who are still in the jungle. They really fear the big wind that comes in the night and goes like this: *hooooooo, hooooo, hooooo.*

There were so many things in the woods that were bad. We didn't know the civilized people. We didn't know if we came out to them whether it would be good or not. For that reason the jungle was sweet to us. It's the same for the Pig People. They are afraid of us here and afraid of the civilized people, so the jungle is sweet to them. They feel safe deep in the jungle.

For us it was the place where we were at home, and it was good for us. Now we are with you missionaries. It's very good to be here with the civilized, especially now that we have God's Word. We will never go back to live all the time in the jungle again.

We've heard that some of the civilized want us to go back and live in the jungle again as we used to; but we can't go back now and drink water potatoes for water, for they will make us sick and even kill us.

Since we've been with the civilized it's so good that we have heard God's Word; we never heard it before. We were afraid to come out because we had so many fears. Now we've heard God's Word, the good news of Jesus. We don't fear anymore because we can see that we have eternal life.

I was a chief before, but the Indians were not afraid of us. My father was a chief too, but the Ayores were not afraid of him. He was a "real" chief but very good. I'll tell you about some good chiefs. Pacade was a real good chief; he didn't bawl out the people. In a battle he killed someone. Another good one was Tadisei, but a snake killed him. He just killed the civilized and didn't bawl out his people.

A chief that was really bad was Abaode; he was really bad. There was a lot of chiefs. We did what they wanted us to do. They said, "Why don't you bring my 'insides' directions?" [Why don't you do my bidding?] Then we did what they said. They would lead us into all kinds of bad things. We did whatever they did, all their sins.

Our chief from back then was Caduide who is here now. He was a very important chief; but they were really mean back then. They were like Uegai who was a big chief, and they destroyed a lot of Ayores in their villages. They killed other unrelated groups too. Caduide killed his own child; I saw him kill him. The boy was about two or three years old; he really killed him. He was crazy.

Uejai killed children, even though their mama and daddy were alive. He killed them when the parents weren't around and then put the body in the path where the father would see it when he returned. They were really mean, like that one Disiejoide, who died a good while back at the old mission station at Cerro Leon. He killed his own child too; it was just crawling. He killed it by hitting him with his forearm till it died. Then they buried him. Disiejoide's victims were many, Ayores and civilized, lots of them. He also killed his own people in his own village. There were many chiefs, and they didn't have any sense.

They don't kill each other any more because they have heard the good news of Jesus. These days are better than the old days. The old days were really bad when our people killed each other.

The bird-god killed us too in the olden days. The bird also "hit" the girl here, called Irangue. It made her bones in her legs bad, but missionary Joyce Buchegger gave her shots and healed her. The bird-god made some Ayores have big boils that suppurated. Our people were really afraid of those boils in the jungle in those days. Some of them died from them. The bird-god afflicted others so that you could hear rumblings from their insides, and they died. There were so many ways that she [the bird] afflicted our people. They were really afraid of her then, and we too, in this generation, really feared her.

They formerly had a time in the jungle where they had to worship the bird. Before daylight they left, and when it became light they blew on their whistles as they went—*hoonooo, hooonooo, hooonooo.* They were really afraid, lest the women and children look at them, which was forbidden. They left and a little later they made camp in the woods, away from the main camp. The young boys (who had carried the things) gave the men's things to them, and the men went looking for honey. The women were afraid, and they didn't look at them or allow the little children to look. The women stayed in the village. The young boys stayed in the men's camp while they were gone, but they didn't play around for fear of punishment by the bird.

After that the men could go back to the village with the women and talk with them; but first they and the women had to make crosses out of cactus wood. The crosses were placed between the two camps. Then the men could go to their regular camp. However, the men were on one side and the women on the other. The bird, Asojna, wouldn't bother them then, because she was afraid of the crosses.

But we don't want the bird any more. We quit after the missionaries came to us.

16

SO TRIBE

THAILAND

The So tribe is of the Mon Khmen language group and several hundred years ago migrated into what is now Thailand from China and Laos. There are more than thirty thousand So here in the northeastern part of Thailand, and up to one hundred thousand more in Laos. (There are a number of the Mon Khmen people in Vietnam who speak languages closely related to So, but we do not know of any So people that far east.)

One interesting thing about the So is that the dialectic changes are very minimal. The So people raise rice for their staple food, but forage in the woods and streams for the things that they eat with their rice.

The So people until very recently were almost completely self-sufficient, relying on other groups for a few trade goods, including knives and clay bowls.

They grew their own cotton, made their own string, and wove their own cloth. Although today they depend on buying many items from the merchants in the area, their life-style would change very little if those things were no longer available.

They still plow with water buffalo, as they have for hundreds of years, and the two-wheeled oxcart is their means of hauling lumber or rice. They live in wooden frame houses built five to six feet off the ground—on poles—and their homes are made of hand-sawn lumber.

The So worship the spirits of their ancestors and still rely basically on the local witch doctor to locate the cause of sickness—an offended spirit—and effect a cure, usually a sacrifice of a chicken or pig.

LOI YONGBANTHOM

Hello, my name is Mr. Loi Yongbanthom; I live with my wife and three daughters in house number 230, in the village of Kusuman, Sakon Nakhon province, here in Thailand.

My wife and I have our faith and trust in Jesus Christ, who is the creator of everything, the owner of heaven, and the Savior of the world. We enjoy singing songs about our faith together, and studying God's Word. We know that we belong to Him and look forward to spending eternity with Him in the place that He is preparing for those who love Him.

However, it wasn't always like that. My people worship spirits; those spirits are everywhere around us, so we have to be very careful so as not to offend the spirits in some way. Sometimes the spirits live in wells. At times they live in large trees, on anthills, or in creeks. We try to avoid going there, because we never know when we might offend them, and then they can cause sickness, pain, or even death. It's best not to go where they are; but, if necessary, we are very careful as to what we say and do around them. In the daytime it's not all that bad, but at night we would be found there only in an emergency, because they say that if we should pass through just as the spirit is leaving or coming out, we'd be in trouble for sure.

When we are sick for some length of time, we're quite sure that a spirit has been offended, so we call the witch doctor, and he tells us which spirit was offended and what we have to offer to appease it—at times a shirt or sarong. At other times we must kill a chicken or pig.

We lived in constant fear, and I could never tell all the story here but will tell of one more thing that gives us great fear. In our village there are quite a number of people who eat spirits. No one wants to be a spirit eater, but at times when we're sick and call the witch doctor, he finds that the reason we are sick is that a spirit that eats people wants to live in us. If we refuse, we'll likely die; if we accept, we'll have to eat spirits and kill people to satisfy the spirit that lives in us. We call these people *Mana's*. As I said, there are many *Mana's* in our village, and they have to keep eating spirits or they themselves will die. They prey mostly on the weak or sick. When women have babies, we have to be especially careful, as they like to go under the room where the baby has been born [houses are built up on poles] and eat its spirit. The child then will live only a few short years.

I remember how scared I was when our first daughter was born. It was in the night that she was born, and I was down under the house, standing guard with a small lamp, when I remembered that Jesus said, "I am the light of the world." I was already a believer at that time, so called on Him, and the darkness seemed to just flee away. It was still dark down there, but I sensed His presence, and it didn't seem dark.

Another aspect of my life that I'd like to tell you about is my religion. I have had a religion ever since I was small; in fact, it's the national religion, and we just naturally consider ourselves as Buddhists. The teachings of Buddha are good; they tell us not to lie, steal, or take another man's wife. My only problem was that I couldn't keep the laws. Compared to some folks, I was very good; to others, I was evil. If I didn't do evil of one sort, I did evil of another sort; but in spite of that, I wasn't worried, because I felt that I was good enough. I felt that my good deeds outweighed my bad ones, and that's all that's necessary to escape pain and evil in the next incarnation—or so Buddhism taught.

I bowed down to trees that have been carved into figures of various men, because I believed that those things could help me. I was totally uninterested in any other religion, because I thought I was on the right road.

When some missionaries came to tell the "good news of Jesus Christ," I really couldn't have cared less. You are probably wondering why I became a believer in Jesus Christ, then. That is the question that my relatives and friends keep asking me. At times they even hate me for my faith in Christ.

This was my problem: Buddhism teaches that if you do good, you'll receive good in the next life; if you do evil, you'll receive evil. But I had no way of knowing how much good I had to do to get to heaven, the place of spirits that have no body, so suffer no desires, be it pain or joy or sorrow or happiness. (It is the desire of Buddhists to reach the place of nonexistence.)

I'd find myself lying or stealing or doing some other evil, so then I had to do some good deeds to outweigh the bad. On making that merit, I'd take some money or goods to the temple, as Buddhism teaches, but I never knew just where I was. If anyone would ask me if I knew where I was going when I died, all I could say that it depended on my merit that I had made and the evil that I had done. That was my life.

Why then did I come to believe in Jesus Christ? I met Jesus because there were some people who brought His story to me. After listening to them tell the story from the Word of God, I realized that the way I was going was all wrong, because Christ caused my blind eyes to see the light. I realized for the first time that I had been bowing down to wood, stone, silver, and gold, no more and no less; it had no life, so couldn't help me.

In addition, I began to realize that Jesus was the owner of heaven—everything came from Him. Because of that, I received Jesus as my Savior. Then I began to be certain that this is the only true way, which is able to assure men that they could spend eternity in heaven. This is the way of Jesus. Praise the Lord!

17

PWO KAREN TRIBE

THAILAND

The Karen tribal people live in mountainous areas of Thailand and Burma. The area they cover stretches from Chiengmai in the north to Patchaburi in south Thailand. Within the group there are several subgroups.

In Thailand there are two main groups: northern Pwo and southern Pwo. Mobo's group is the southern Pwo. The dialects are different from those in north Thailand. The Pwo Karen speak a Tibeten-Burmese language, which is tonal. That dialect is spoken from Uthai-Thani in eastern Thailand to Patchaburi in the south.

The population numbers many thousands. They are basically animists, with a veneer of Mon-Buddhism. They live in abject fear of malevolent spirits, whom they constantly have to suppress. Their whole life is wrapped up in seeing that those spirits are taken care of by elaborate ceremonies.

They attribute all sickness and luck to the upsetting of the delicate balance between themselves and the spirits. They have a writing system based on the Mon-alphabet. The Mon tribes were large kingdoms several hundred years ago.

The Karen say their lack of success is based on a lost book that each one of the original family was given. After some time the white foreigner would bring it back to them. When that book comes back, so will peace and happiness.

The Pwo Karen, as a tribe, have had the gospel for many years, but are very resistant to change. One dialect in Burma has had some believers, and up north some have responded.

That particular dialect has been very resistant to the gospel, having only a few believers. Recently there seems to be thaw in the attitude to the gospel. Folks are listening. We pray more will respond. New Tribes Mission has been working with this tribe for about ten years.

Mobo was turned out of his home when he believed. He lived in the family rice-house for a year or two. Now he is living on his own and making his own rice fields, which is proving to be difficult for him because he is not a young man anymore.

Pwo Karen traditions say each original family was given a book, which they lost. A white foreigner is someday to bring the book back, and the peace and happiness will return.

MOBO

In the beginning, before I believed, I had to worship and feed spirits. These spirits were very wicked; they would bite me and fight me. Whenever they bothered me I had to feed them with fruit of the tree and bamboo. I had to find what direction it was bothering me from. At that time my heart was pitch dark.

Now that I am a believer, my liver is bright and my heart is opened. I can build my house wherever and whenever I like. I can travel on whatever day I like, whenever I like. I am ever so happy now that I know that when I die I can go to heaven without having to wander around bothering people when I die.

I am so glad that the foreigners have come to learn my language and tell me about God and pull me back from being bothered by spirits. Now I am happy that God's Spirit lives in me. Buddhism is finished now. We all have to follow the Lord.

18

LAWA TRIBE

THAILAND

The Lawa tribe is one of the Mon-Khmer tribes of southeast Asia. Although the word "Lawa" is used in Thailand to refer to a number of small tribal groups, this report refers to a group of about twelve thousand people in northwestern Thailand, in the provinces of Maehongson and Chiangmai. Their language is nontonal, and is most closely related to the Wa of Burma.

In common with other hill tribes of Thailand, the Lawa make their living largely by slash-and-burn agriculture, with rice as their major crop. Many have begun to make paddy fields in the small streams, but there is not enough level land to support the people except by slash-and-burn agriculture. Cotton is raised, and clothes are woven from homespun yarn. Some of the Lawa are able to make muzzle-loading guns and other iron goods, and to make ornaments of silver. Homes are usually built on poles of wood and bamboo, with a thatch of elephant grass.

Although some of the Lawa have taken on a veneer of Buddhism, for the most part they are animists following the ancestor worship of their forefathers. They make constant sacrifices to appease the hosts of evil spirits who haunt the forests and fields, as well as the village spirits who demand regular offerings and animals, whiskey, vegetables, and so on. A complicated system of superstitions has developed in light of their world view, and magic is practiced by the sorcerers to control the unknown. Sickness is usually blamed on the supernatural.

Missionaries first began to work with the Lawa and to learn their language in 1954. By 1957 some of the people were ready to turn from their old ways. Soon they were able to read their own language, and the first attempts at translation of Scripture and other literature were in their hands. Growth of the Christian community was slow but steady, and by 1979 there were churches in seven villages, each with its own leader. The New Testament was translated and published in 1971, and portions of the Old Testament were added later. The Lawa now support two Christian workers full-time and actively preach the gospel in other areas.

143

Pi Kawng Kaew–"I praise God, for though I am not all I should be, it is He who has helped me to this point."

PI KAWNG KAEW

Praise to God who chose me to come to Himself. A long time ago I was one who did not know God at all. When Christians first came to my village I was much displeased. The message of God seemed true and honest to me, but I would not listen very long. When I heard only a few words, I wanted to get away from it. I said to myself that I could never accept it.

My brother-in-law kept listening to the message and said that he could accept it. But when the missionaries came to visit me I was very angry with them. After a while I became tired of deceiving the missionaries and no longer wanted to see them. So, I pretended to be sick, and put up a *talia* [bamboo star that is used to ward off spirits and also makes the house taboo to strangers], so the missionaries would not visit me.

The missionaries kept getting on my nerves. They studied the language with other Lawa people instead of me, like Uncle Eoe, Hua's father. When they studied with them the dialect was a little different, and they preferred to learn my dialect.

Then missionary [Gene] Nelson said to me, "Even if you put up the *talia*, the spirits can fly over it and get into your house another way." My brother-in-law and I were very angry with him. Now when I think of it, my anger at that time was very evil; it was of the evil spirits for sure.

A long time ago I was a slave of sin of many kinds. I was a gambler and a whiskey drinker; I also smoked opium at times. It was because of those vices that I thought I could not come to trust in God.

When God chose my older sisters' families to come to Him, I was very upset and angry. I said I was a believer in merit making; I trusted in the monks and believed in the way of the temple [Buddhist]. When it was the Thai new year, I greatly wanted to make offerings in the temple.

When I thought of my sisters who had become Christians, I was so upset that it became an obsession with me. I became mentally deranged because of it. I went to the temples. I made gifts to old people [a way of gaining merit]; I spent all I had. Then I was completely crazy and no longer had control of my mind. I went into people's homes and acted angry toward them. Everyone was afraid of me.

They locked me in jail. I thank God for those who came to visit me in jail and proclaimed the gospel of God to me there. At that time there were not many Lawa who believed in God. It was some of the Karens, like Khroo Mayta and others, who came to see me in jail and prayed for me.

After a while I got a little better and got out of jail. Then I went crazy again, worse than the first time. My mother had not yet discarded the spirits. After that my mother threw out all the spirits in our house, all fetishes and symbols of spirit worship. After mother got rid of all the spirits and people prayed for me, the prayers were effective.

I began to have faith [in Christ] while I was yet in the jail. When I came out of jail I wanted to be baptized right away. I received a new breath [heart], which is renewed continually until now. I praise God, for though I am not all I should be, it is He who has helped me to this point.

Mr. Kawng Kaew is about forty-five years old and has been a Christian for about twenty years. He is a deacon in the Lawa church in Maesarieng, active in witnessing to people of several languages (Thai, Karen, Lawa). He is a farmer and also travels, selling home remedies in the mountain villages in order to be able to witness for Christ.

NAWI KAEWSAI

A long time ago we were in the hands of the spirits. It was really hard for us. It was truly painful what we had to go through because of what the spirits did to us. Those spirits caused us to have much trouble; they tormented our bodies. If we did not go and seek pigs and chickens for them, they would not let us get well. We had to find a witch doctor, cook rice for him, and beg him to come and eat it. It was so hard for us.

At that time I was a person who had a very big spirit tormenting me. It made me have much suffering. Every month that evil spirit came to me; at the full moon and at the new moon it came to me. Now I am free from the spirits, because of God.

Another thing, we were poor. My husband was a sick man; from the time when we had only two children, he was sick. Even though he was sick like that, still it was necessary to feast the spirits, necessary to go searching for the things to feed them.

We had to go to Karen villages to buy animals to sacrifice. I had to hunt in the forest for leaves with which to make mats to sell. I had to sell my clothes that I had woven and all of my necklaces and silver bracelets to buy the required sacrifices.

Now, I truly thank God to be free from spirits like that. I have received unhindered breath [a peaceful, unburdened heart] because of trusting God. The grace of God, which He gave me, is so great.

I was terribly poor at the time, before I believed in God; I had to beg from the homes of other people. Now I am not rich either, but I have a happy breath [heart] because of God.

No matter how things go, I am happy. Whether we are sick or well, even though we are in need, we can still rejoice because of God. We have no other pressure or trouble. We thank God for giving us joy and peace. When I see other people in trouble, I am deeply concerned for them because I have found joy in trusting in God. I cannot help them myself, but I pray for God to help them. I cannot lift their burden, but He can.

Thank God for helping our family, every one of us. There are six children; we have dedicated them to God, all six of them from their childhood. Now some of them are serving God, even if not all yet. They have joy in serving Him. In all the things of this world there is nothing as great as to have my children serving God. Now I have unhindered breath in knowing that two of my sons are serving God. We truly thank God who gives us happiness in this.

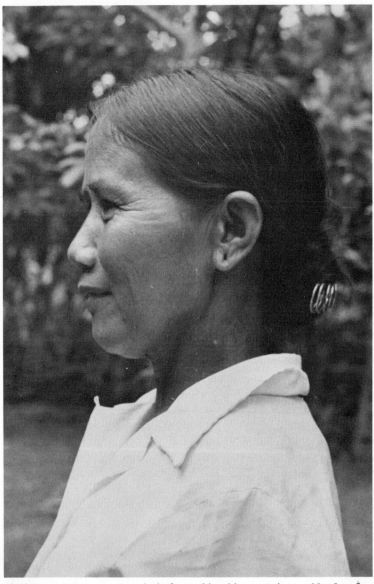

Nawi Kaewsai–"I was a person who had a very big spirit tormenting me. Now I am free from the spirits, because of God."

In all the world there is nothing to compare with the gospel of God. Though people have cars or water buffaloes, or oxen, or rice fields, those things are not comparable to believing in God. Praise the Lord!

Two of Mrs. Kaewsai's sons are in the ministry, serving the Lawa churches as teachers of the Bible and also visiting in villages where there are no believers. She is about fifty years old, has learned to read as an adult, and is an active leader of the women's work in the Maesarieng church.

The family first turned to Christ out of heathenism about twenty-two years ago. Mr. Kaewsai serves as an elder in a Lawa church and was the main informant for translation of the Lawa New Testament.

"Now we are free because of Jesus." Kham Chainit is an elder in the Lawa Maesarieng church of Northwest Thailand.

KHAM CHAINIT

Formerly we were believers in the evil spirits. When I believed that way it was very hard for me, but we did not know what to do. When we were sick we had to go to the diviners. We had to feast the spirits and call back our soul stuff [a ceremony to restore health by calling back a straying inner self]. It was necessary to do all that in order for the sick person to get well. It was certainly difficult. When we found that difficulty we didn't know what to do.

Afterward we heard about the gospel of God. We heard how Jesus could deliver people from the power of the spirits; therefore, we were willing to believe. The gospel of Jesus has truly given us joy and peace. It is Jesus who saves us from sin. When people came and preached the gospel of God to us it was really a benefit to us, the Lawa people. The old ways were hard indeed.

What was hard? It was the way of the evil spirits that was hard for us. Now we are free from that way. We know the story of new life. New life does not come from human sources; it comes from God. It was God who caused missionaries to come and preach to us, telling us how to be free because of Jesus.

We thank Jesus who was willing to die for us. We are sinners. If we were not sinners, He would not need to die. Now we are set free from sin and free too from the difficult ways we used to have. There is no other way to be free except by the way of Jesus; that is the only way. It is by our faith that we can be free from the old difficult ways.

When we speak of the old difficult ways of divining, it is like this, that is so hard. When we went to divine we had to pick up some kernels of hulled rice. Then we would have the sick person spit on them. When he had spit on the rice, we would take it to the diviner. Then he would ask for a sign [a consecutive series of either odd or even numbers or rice kernels would indicate which spirit was to be feasted]. When he received the sign, sometimes it was necessary to get a white chicken. If there were none in our village we would be forced to go to a Karen village somewhere. We had to search until we got the proper-sized white chicken. Sometimes it had to be a duck. If we didn't have one in our house, we had to go searching for it. That was what was hard in feasting the spirits.

It was necessary to go to Karen villages and Thai villages far away. That was hard. In divining sometimes we had to get a sorcerer. Many times there was no one in our village. Then we had to go and call one from a distant village. If we called a sorcerer it cost a lot of cowry shells and money. He would not come free; we had to hire him; without wages he would not come to us. He would not ask for wages, of course; he would have us make him an offering in a basket. His offerings sometimes cost thirty Baht, but sometimes it would be forty or fifty Baht [at present a day's wages for the Lawa is often less than twenty Baht].

The offering had to have a string of forest beads and also candles and cotton yarn. We had to go and search for each item. If anything was missing, the sorcerer would not do it for us. Also it had to have rice and whiskey. If it was a spirit on the main trail, we had to have a Karen sorceror and do a Karen ceremony. It took two chickens, and the chants had to be in the Karen language.

We had to divine and find out whether we had to use a Karen or a Thai or a Lawa sorcerer. If it was a Karen sorcerer, we had to use a chicken's thigh bone; sometimes we used an egg. We put the egg in a cup and could see what spirit it was in the egg.

The sorcerer knew by what he saw in the egg. Using a chicken bone, he would say, "If he will live, let the stick turn upward; if he will die, let it go down." He blows on a stick and says, "If the stick breaks, the person will die; if it stays whole, he will live."

That was what was hard for us, the Lawa people. Divining is really difficult, the worship of spirits. We have no other way to be free from these hard things. Besides the way of Jesus, we find no other way to escape.

Other people often say, "If you believe in Jesus, a giant will devour you." There aren't really any giants. It is the spirits that are difficult to us [a play on words here; "giant" and "difficult" are the same word]. Now we are free. Free by what? Free because of Jesus.

Mr. Chainit, about fifty years old, has been a Christian for more than twenty years. He is the father of four daughters. He works as a gardener and serves as an elder in the Lawa Maesarieng church of Northwest Thailand. Born in the mountain village of Forest town, he moved to the valley area as a young man.

19

THE BATTLE OF THE AGES

Ever since the church began, Satan has been warring against God's program. (Imagine Satan marshaling his demons, giving them a pep talk: *"Stop world evangelization."*) And the war has been raging ever since against those who in obedience to God's Word are working to reach people for Christ.

Missions have always suffered because of Satan's attacks. Persecution is not something new. Tribal people have killed and maimed missionaries who had gone to them to tell of Christ and His power to save them.

Other religions have fought hard to stop the gospel. Jails have housed some pioneers of the faith in foreign mission fields. The enemy tries in many ways to discourage missionaries so they will go home.

In 1943, five fine young men, missionaries to Bolivia, were killed by the Ayore tribe. Those men had gone to tell them of Christ, who could give them peace. The missionaries were dead and buried before they had been in Bolivia a year. Later, someone else told the Ayore of the Lord Jesus, and today there is a living church among those people.

Some twelve years later, five other missionaries were killed by the Auca tribe in the jungles of Ecuador. Communication (or the lack of it) no doubt contributed to that incident.

Dave Yarwood gave his life on the bank of a river in Bolivia. He had gone with a few other men to reach natives with the gospel. He was never able to do it, because he died before learning the Nambecuara language.

Within the last decade, we have read about what happened in the Congo. Rhodesia had the most recent brutal killing that has been documented; a number of missionaries were killed.

The list grows long. Many missionaries have spilled their blood on some lonesome, isolated spots, far from civilization as we know it. Yet missionaries go on, and new recruits continue to give their lives to take the gospel to a lost world.

The Bible tells us that *all* have sinned (Romans 3:23). It does not matter what color, nation, rank, or position one has. The heathen are lost. That is a biblical fact and not open to debate.

The tribal people need to hear the gospel, the good news of Jesus Christ, in order to be saved. Just as civilized Americans must believe in Christ to be saved, so must the unreached pagans. The gospel is the power of God unto salvation (Romans 1:16). Faith comes by hearing, and hearing by the Word of God (Romans 10:17). So, the unreached tribes must hear the gospel before they can believe. That is why thousands of missionaries are preaching the gospel around the world today.

In Revelation 5:9 we read, "And they sung a new song, saying, Thou art worthy to take the book, and to open the seals thereof: for thou wast slain, and hast redeemed us to God by thy blood *out of every kindred, and tongue, and people, and nation*" (italics added).

It is evident that some from every tribe in the world will be in heaven when that prophecy is fulfilled. For those people to be a part of that company, they have to hear the gospel, so missionaries must go to tell them.

Is it any wonder that Satan is attacking missions?

It is good to know that God's Word makes clear that His plan will be completed. Communists can threaten, false religions can infiltrate, and the media can discredit God's servants, but the opponents are fighting for a lost cause. Jesus said, "I will build my church, and the gates of hell shall not prevail against it" (Matthew 16:18). For that promise we are very grateful.

There is no reason for us to be discouraged. Really, we are encouraged. Satan only fights those who are doing what God wants done.

Are the tribal people really happy the way they are? Should the missionary go home?

It is the hope of this author that this testimonial of what the grace of God means to tribal people—who have heard of Jesus Christ and His love and have responded by believing in Him—will convince you of the truth.

They have shared their hearts with you. They have told of the joy they now know as born-again Christians. They need your prayers, as do we. There are others who live yet in fear and without hope. They never will know true peace—will never be saved—until they hear the gospel of our Lord Jesus Christ.

20

A PERSONAL WORD

In 1977 I was interviewed by a reporter for a radio station in Philadelphia. The reason for that interview was a book that had just been published entitled *Genocide in Paraguay*. The mission home office had asked if I would answer the interviewer's questions regarding the tribal situation in Paraguay, because I had lived there for many years and was knowledgeable of what had happened.

The first question the reporter asked was interesting. "What are your credentials?" she asked. "What entitles you to answer the questions I'm about to ask with regard to activity among tribal people in Paraguay?" I thought the question was an intelligent one. After all, if the truth is going to be heard, the credibility of the spokesman is important.

Why had someone not asked the writers of all those sensational articles that question? Their stories were sold to several magazines and newspapers around the world. They were then printed as though they were true.

I asked the editor of the Sunday supplement of a major newspaper in Miami, Florida, "Why didn't you check up on the truth of the article before you printed it?" Do you know what his answer was? "We trust the London press source." He admitted he did not know the author, yet without question the article was printed as truth.

Now I was being questioned by the reporter as to my ability to answer her questions intelligently. I told her I had lived in Paraguay for many years, traveled the country quite extensively, represented our mission to the Paraguayan government, flown many thousands of miles over Paraguayan soil, translated the Scripture into an Indian language, and so forth. She interrupted me by saying, "My, you must be an authority on Indian affairs in Paraguay."

My first reaction was to laugh and react by saying, "No, I'm certainly no expert." But then I went on to say, "Wait a minute. If you are to compare me with any of the authors of those articles, and especially with the author of the book in question, *Genocide in Paraguay*, yes, I am an expert. The man who wrote that book had not even been in the country, yet he wrote as though he were an authority on the subject. His credentials were a little less than adequate, and the manuscript was consequently completely lacking in credibility."

In 1949 our family of five went to Paraguay to help pioneer a new field for New Tribes Mission. We were residents of Paraguay until 1972. Since that time I have returned to our adopted country. It was our home for many years, the place where our children were raised and where two of our sons were born.

The Lord gave us love for the tribes we worked and lived with. Since the Lengua and Sanapana language are quite similar and all of the Sanapana tribe speak the Lengua language, we learned Lengua.

The Lord blessed His Word as we preached it, and many of both tribes came to know Christ as their own personal Savior.

The believers were taught to go out and teach others. We saw the Lord multiply the lives of several of those simple Indian men. Teaching the Word to those people was a joy. They seemed to soak it up like a sponge. Then, as the Spirit of God worked in their lives, they themselves went out to distant places to preach the gospel to their own people, where it had not yet gone.

For the believers to grow, they needed the New Testament in their language. The gospels had already been translated, but the rest of the New Testament still had to be translated in order for them to have it in its complete form.

I worked with various Indian informants for over fifteen years, off and on, before it was completed. What a thrill to see the joy in the Indians' eyes. Imagine, after all those years they finally had in their language a complete New Testament under one cover. They were thrilled!

The experience was an education for me as we worked day in and day out, trying under God to do the very best job of translating His Word into a tribal language. We needed to be careful to make it understandable, something that would speak to their hearts in a dynamic way.

For me, it had been a time of mixed emotions. There were times of frustrations, mixed with thrill! Frustration when things did not go right; thrill when a chapter was completed, to the obvious joy of the tribe. Years of labor in translation do not qualify one as an expert in Indian affairs, but go a long way in impressing the Christians who care that what we say has credibility.

For years we have handled the area of governmental representation for the mission. Several times a year it was necessary to visit the missionaries working in other areas among other tribes. Sometimes the work was one of pioneering from the very beginning. Occasionally it meant looking for hostile tribes; again, at other times the tribes were semi-civilized, such as the Manjui tribe in western Paraguay.

Over the years, the experience we have gained has given an insight into many different cultures. We have found that no two cultures are exactly the same. What one tribe may call wrong may be perfectly all right with another group. Their world views differ. Their value systems vary from one extreme to another.

The past six years have taken us to all of our South American fields and Africa. First Panama, then Venezuela, Brazil, Paraguay, Bolivia, Colombia, and Mexico. For the past six years Africa has been on our itinerary five times. My colleagues in Senegal and I have surveyed several tribes, to evaluate whether or not we ought to be involved in reaching them. Some tribes have no gospel witness at all; others do have missionaries working with them. We had to determine, in light of need, where our missionaries should go first.

For well over thirty years our lives have been given over completely to that objective. We have involved ourselves in reaching the unreached tribal people with the gospel of Jesus Christ.

Those are our credentials. Let us state some facts that we have learned during the past quarter of a century:

Each tribe has its own culture. In some ways one tribe may be similar to another, but in many ways they differ completely.

All tribes we have ever known anything about have their own religions. Some are animists; some tribes have shamans, or witch doctors. Their religions differ, but they do have some form of worship.

All tribes have one thing in common in their paganism. Their religion leaves them without hope; they all live in fear; they are all unhappy in their paganism.

When Christ changes those people's lives, they have hope; they have joy, and that becomes evident in their facial expressions as well as in their way of life, not to mention the testimonials from their own lips. We have lived to see the changes take place and know whereof we speak.